GOSPEL-POWERED
humility

GOSPEL-POWERED

humility

WILLIAM P. FARLEY

P U B L I S H I N G

P.O. BOX 817 • PHILLIPSBURG • NEW JERSEY 08865-0817

Unless otherwise indicated, Scripture quotations are from *ESV Bible* ® (*The Holy Bible, English Standard Version* ®). Copyright © 2001 by Crossway Bibles, a publishing ministry of Good News Publishers. Used by permission. All rights reserved.

Scripture quotations marked (NIV) are from the HOLY BIBLE, NEW INTERNATIONAL VERSION®. NIV®. Copyright © 1973, 1978, 1984 by International Bible Society. Used by permission of Zondervan Publishing House. All rights reserved.

Scripture quotations marked (NLT) are taken from the Holy Bible, New Living Translation, copyright 1996, 2004. Used by permission of Tyndale House Publishers, Inc., Wheaton, Illinois 60189. All rights reserved.

Italics within Scripture quotations indicate emphasis added.

Printed in the United States of America

Library of Congress Cataloging-in-Publication Data

Farley, William P., 1948-
  Gospel-powered humility / William P. Farley.
      p. cm.
  Includes bibliographical references.
  ISBN 978-1-59638-240-4 (pbk.)
  1. Humility–Religious aspects–Christianity. I. Title.
  BV4647.H8F37 2011
  241'.4–dc23
                                          2011031307

Pride Is Utter Poverty of Soul Disguised as Riches,
Imaginary Light Where in Fact There Is Darkness.
—**John Climacus** (570–649)

How foolish, how absurd, how ruinous, how blindly destructive of its own object, does pride appear! By attempting to soar, it only plunges itself in the mire; and, while endeavoring to erect for itself a throne, it undermines the ground on which it stands, and digs its own grave.

It plunged Satan from heaven into hell; it banished our first parents from paradise, and it will, in a similar manner, ruin all, who indulge it. It keeps us in ignorance of God, shuts us out from his favor, prevents us from resembling him, deprives us, in this world, of all the honor and happiness, which communion with him would confer; and in the next, unless previously hated, repented of, and renounced, will bar forever against us the door of heaven, and close upon us the gates of hell.

O, then, my friends beware, above all things, beware of pride. Beware, lest you indulge it imperceptibly; for it is, perhaps, of all sins, the most secret, subtle, and insinuating. That you may detect it, remember, that he only, who seeks after God in his appointed way, is humble; and that all who neglect thus to seek him, are most certainly proud in heart, and, consequently, an abomination unto the Lord.

—Edward Payson (1783–1827)

Contents

Preface

WHAT DO AUGUSTINE, William Law, Jonathan Edwards, Andrew Murray, and C. S. Lewis all have in common? Two things: First, they concur that humility is the root of all virtue. It is the essential spiritual fruit, the one necessary for both conversion and sanctification. Second, they agree that despite its importance, it is the least emphasized virtue. "Generally speaking," noted William Law (1686–1761), "it is the least understood, the least regarded, the least intended, the least desired and sought after, of all other virtues, amongst all sorts of Christians."[1]

Since Law wrote these words in the eighteenth century, little has changed. We are in the same quagmire today. The most important virtue is still the least valued. Dr. Stuart Scott, writing in 2002, notes, "Despite the fact that [pride] is so widespread, it is perplexing how little has been written on pride in recent years. To read very much on the subject of pride, one must read Puritan literature."[2] In the secular world, humility is seen as weakness, a lack of confidence, a virtue that impedes advancement or productivity. Many in the church share these assumptions.

The truth is the opposite. Failure to prioritize humility impoverishes our efforts to evangelize, retards our growth in godliness, and impedes the effectiveness of our ministries. And it makes us ineffective in business.

If humility matters this much, then Christian ministry should aim to produce not just faith, but a faith that humbles sinners. That God has designed the gospel to do just this is often not understood. Why and how God designed the gospel to promote humility is the subject of this book.

PROBLEM AND SOLUTION

The absence of an emphasis on pride and humility is costly. Dr. Jim Edwards writes, "American Christianity is suffering theological collapse. The primary commitments of church members seem to be peace, the search for personal fulfillment, and the conviction that God judges no one."[3] David Wells adds, "For many people, the word 'evangelical' has become a synonym for what is trite, superficial, and moneygrubbing, a byword for what has gone wrong with Protestantism."[4] To prove this conclusion, Wells later notes, "In America 45 percent say they are born again but only 9 percent, and maybe only 7 percent, give any evidence of Christian seriousness by way of minimal biblical knowledge for making life's decisions."[5]

One reason for this is that many of our pulpits have lost their cutting edge. The clarion call to flee the wrath of God has almost disappeared. This message feels old-fashioned—language that doesn't jibe with the modern world. Instead, we hear sermons on how to have a better marriage, how to manage our finances, and how to have better relationships. Yes, these subjects matter greatly—but they are secondary, not primary. They are not theology. They are the *fruits* of theology. They are not the gospel. They are *fruits* of the gospel. When we assume the gospel and pursue the fruits, the fruits eventually displace the gospel and all that remains is "moralism." When this happens, grace degenerates into "being nice," God's love becomes superheated human affection, and his mercy is a tip of God's hat to "decent people" who try hard.

The remedy for all of this is the doctrine of God, and God reveals himself most clearly in the most basic Christian truth, the gospel. My contention is that the church is most apt to fulfill its God-given purpose when we preach the gospel in such a way that it produces a faith that humbles sinner and saint alike.

This book is my attempt to fortify the gospel we preach. In it the reader will learn that one of the first signs of pride is the secret feeling that I am really humble, in fact more humble than most, whereas people growing in humility deeply feel the pain of their pride.

You will also learn why apathy toward God's Word is often a symptom of pride, and that the pursuit of humility is the cure.

The reader will learn that humility is a necessary precedent for both justification and sanctification. You may also be surprised to learn that Romans 1–3 contains seven words about the bad news for every word announcing the good news, and there is an important reason for this. You will also discover that justification by faith alone is a humbling doctrine and that God designed it that way for a specific purpose.

You will learn why God's wrath is an expression of his goodness, why you would not be able to trust him if he did not become intensely angry with sin and sinners.

You will find out how preachers from past generations wielded the bad news to amplify the beauty of God's infinite goodness, and obtained remarkable long-term results.

You will see why the humble are able to discern what God is doing, even while the proud are blind to the activity of God's Spirit.

WHY ANOTHER BOOK ON HUMILITY?

In the last century, several excellent books on humility have been published. Andrew Murray's classic, *Humility, the Beauty of Holiness*, published at the end of the nineteenth century, is one example. More recent decades have added Wayne Mack's *Humility: The Forgotten Virtue*, Thomas Jones and Michael Fontenot's *The Prideful Soul's Guide to Humility*, and C. J. Mahaney's *Humility: True Greatness*. Each volume does an excellent job of describing why humility matters and how to acquire it. So why another book on humility?

Answer: This book takes the reader beyond the personal benefits of humility. It agrees with these authors and then builds on them. Humility is the crucial virtue. Without it, the Christian will not be fruitful. Humility is the fertilizer that nourishes our souls and makes us fruitful. Without it, we will lack zeal, be unable to mourn sin, and have little compassion and patience for others. In short, without the pursuit of humility, our souls will wither.

In addition, this book asserts that unless we preach the gospel with the intention of humbling sinners, there will be few real conversions, and among those who are converted the fruit will be withered.

There is a three-foot-high door in the front of our local Walmart. It looks like a door for the vertically challenged. Curious about its purpose, I inquired of one of the employees. "We return shopping carts through that door." As he answered, I realized that this mini-door symbolized God's kingdom. The kingdom of God is for those vertically challenged in a spiritual sense. You must stoop to enter. You must humble yourself. God opposes the proud, but he gives grace to the humble. Therefore, faith that does not provoke humility, causing it to sprout and grow, is unlikely to be a saving faith, no matter how many times the individual signs a card or responds to an altar call.

WHY THIS BOOK?

That is why I wrote this book. If humility is this essential, it makes sense that God has designed the gospel to produce a faith that humbles the proud. This book contends that he has. Those who understand this principle wield the gospel purposely. First they let it humble themselves. Then they use it to produce a faith that humbles their hearers. They preach the gospel differently. They conduct Christian ministry differently.

There is an old saying from the seventies: "The job of the church is to disturb the comfortable and comfort the disturbed." Rephrased in biblical language, we could say: "Our job is to humble the proud (for the proud are always comfortable, complacent, unconcerned about their spiritual condition) and comfort the humble (for only the humble are ready for the comfort that the gospel brings)." Charles Simeon (1759–1836) understood this principle. Here is how he described the three aims of his ministry: "To humble the sinner, to exalt the Saviour, and to promote holiness."[6] Few contemporary Christians share these aims, and that is one significant reason for the predicament of modern evangelicalism. Simeon's assumptions are those of a bygone era, and the spirit of our age blows hard against those who attempt to return there. Yet this is our need. God has designed the gospel to humble sinners, exalt Christ, and produce the holiness that is always the fruit of those who seek humility first.

The first two chapters argue that humility is the chief and necessary virtue, the virtue that precedes the others. They lay the groundwork for all that follows.

Chapters 3–7 constitute the main body of this book. They argue from church history and the first three chapters of Romans that the apostolic gospel seeks to produce a humbling faith. Presuming that fallen man's default condition is pride, that pride is the backbone of original sin, and that it is the great barrier to the gospel, Paul began his "gospel presentation"[7] with the bad news. He knew that pride was the great barrier to conversion, so he sought to humble sinners. More importantly, a careful analysis of Romans 1–3 indicates that

13

the vast majority of Paul's gospel presentation was bad news. It concerned the wrath of God, the inevitability of judgment, and the utter sinfulness of man. Only then did Paul introduce the good news—justification by faith alone—and he did so in order that no one might "boast" (Rom. 3:19, 27). By contrast, the time spent on the good news was short.

Chapters 8 and 9 apply the thesis to the work of ministry. Chapter 8 discusses the fundamental sin that keeps us from using Paul's methods: the fear of man. Chapter 9 ends the book with an exhortation to the Christian worker to model the humility that he or she seeks to produce in others.

TARGET AUDIENCE

This is a book for everyone doing Christian ministry, not just those paid by the church. It is for those who want to share the gospel with unbelievers more effectively. It is for those who want to counsel their friends more productively. It is also for professional Christian counselors. Most importantly, it is for those who regularly preach the Word of God. Preaching is the rudder that steers the local church. He who preaches to produce humility will increasingly steer his church into the deep waters of God's holiness. His evangelistic efforts will be fruitful. That is because the power of God pursues the ministry that seeks to humble others.

We have already noted that humility is not the goal of most Christian workers. A random survey of the sermons of some of our largest churches will quickly convince one that the subjects most apt to provoke humility are conspicuously absent. Sermons on the sinfulness of sin, the terrors of hell, the reality of final judgment, the fear of God, the substitutionary penal atonement, and the wrath of God are exceedingly rare. Instead of disturbing the comfortable, we seek to comfort them further. Instead of humbling sinners, we seek to further inflate their self-esteem. God will be glorified, grace will be truly amazing, and Christians will experience true spiritual happiness and contentment to the degree that our egos have been joyfully deflated.

My fervent hope is that this book will do something to remedy this problem.

Acknowledgments

I WANT TO ACKNOWLEDGE and thank some old, dead, white men whose thoughts have provided the creative spark for this book.

My relationship with them began in the summer of 1987. At the time I was wrestling with the attributes of God. How can God be wrathful and loving at the same time? How is it possible for God to be both infinitely just and infinitely merciful? The Bible presented me with a God who was all of these and more, but I was not prepared to answer these questions by throwing part of my Bible out.

About this time I came across *A Harmony of the Divine Attributes* by William Bates, D.D. (1625–99), a Puritan. The thesis of his book was that the cross was the place where the love of God and wrath of God shook hands; the justice of God and the mercy of God lay down together; and the righteousness of God found fulfillment in the grace of God. It was a personal watershed. Since that time the cross of Christ has been at the center of my thinking.

In God's providence Bates was shortly followed by my first reading of Jonathan Edwards' (1703–58) *Dissertation on the End for Which God Created the World*. This was another personal turning point. For the first time I beheld the centrality, the magnificence, and the awful immensity of God. My man-centered worldview transitioned to a God-centered perspective that has only grown over the years. The greatness and glory of the God

17

understood by Edwards captured my imagination. A process of personal humbling began for which I am deeply grateful. For five years I devoured the works of Edwards in my spare time.

For these men and others like them (Bunyan, Spurgeon, Lloyd-Jones) I am deeply grateful to God. In his kindness he has provided them to humble me and the arrogance of modern life.

To their memory I dedicate this book.

In addition, I want to thank David Farley and David Nelson for painstakingly reading this manuscript and providing critique. However, for all the mistakes and eccentricities in this work I take full responsibility.

THE PROBLEM

Humility "is so essential to the right state of our souls, that there is no pretending to a reasonable or pious life without it. We may as well think to see without eyes, or live without breath, as to live in the spirit of religion without the spirit of humility. And although it is thus the soul and essence of all religious duties, yet is it, generally speaking, the least understood, the least regarded, the least intended, the least desired and sought after, of all other virtues, amongst all sorts of Christians."

—William Law (1686–1761), A Devout Call[1]

1

"There It Is"

"Alas, how much pride have the best of us in our hearts!
It is the worst part of the body of sin and death, the
first sin that ever entered into the universe, and the last
that is rooted out. It is God's most stubborn enemy!"
—Jonathan Edwards[1] (1703–58)

A FEW YEARS AGO, I decided to conduct a Bible study for
a group of singles. I gave them a list of topics to rate in order
of their greatest need. The results were a pleasant surprise.
Rejecting practical teaching such as how to forgive, 80 percent wanted greater intimacy with Christ. Their response was
consistent with my experience over the years.

Although the practice of spiritual disciplines and servanthood should lead us into a deeper experience of our
union with Christ, these disciplines will not, by themselves,
do so. Knowledge of the Bible, prayer, worship, and witnessing should all deepen our relationship with God. We engage
in these practices to please God and love our fellow man,
but pleasing God and loving people won't happen unless we

add one crucial virtue to the mix. Of the importance of this virtue I was ignorant for many years.

EYES OPENED

God opened my eyes in a dramatic way. In October 1993, during my Bible study, Isaiah 66:2 graphically caught my attention: "This is the one I esteem: he who is humble and contrite in spirit, and trembles at my word" (NIV). I wanted a deeper relationship with God, and I felt convinced that this verse had something to do with it, but I did not understand why. So I prayed, "Lord, help me understand what this verse has to do with a deeper relationship with you."

Five days later my wife and I were leaving Cannon Beach, Oregon, for a drive down the Oregon coast. While I was meditating on the thirteenth chapter of 1 Corinthians, my attention was caught by a second verse: "Now I know in part; then I shall know fully, even as I am fully known" (1 Cor. 13:12 NIV). Instinctively, I sensed that God *saw* spiritual darkness in me to which I was blind, that God loved me despite this spiritual cancer, and that someday he would let me see it as he saw it, but I didn't know what the cancer was. So again I prayed, "God, please open my eyes to this hidden evil."

As we drove south, I tried to make the connection between Isaiah 66:2 and 1 Corinthians 13:12. So I prayed a third time: "God, show me how these verses fit together. What do they mean for me?"

A few minutes later, my wife began talking about a movie she liked. Irritated by her insertion of such a trivial topic into my important meditation, I condescendingly criticized her and the movie. Instantly, three life-changing words knifed deep into my conscious thought. They weren't audible, but they came so suddenly and were so completely nonvolitional that I literally lurched behind the steering wheel.

22

"THERE IT IS!"

"What was that?" I thought in wonder.

And then, recognizing that God had spoken to me,[2] I asked, "What is *IT*?"

Next an overwhelming sense of the moral ugliness of *IT*, the arrogance and pride with which I had just spoken to Judy, washed over me. In an instant I saw this sin through God's eyes, in God's light. For the first time I saw and felt about my pride as did God. I felt God's hatred of my arrogance.

The next sensation was a profound conviction that despite the presence of this sin, God had loved me. For forty-five years I had been the poster boy for this sin, and yet God had loved me anyway. For a brief second I knew Bill Farley as *God* knew me. It was painful and wonderful at the same time. I saw my pride as God saw it. It was repulsive. Then I wept tears of joy as I saw God's indescribable love for one so unworthy.

Those three words radically changed my life. It was a huge turning point. I was permanently changed. Once home, I began to study Isaiah 66:2. The pages that follow are the fruit of this ongoing study.

The bottom line is this: The indispensable virtue, the one needed for intimacy with God and all spiritual fruitfulness, is humility—what Jesus also called being "poor in spirit" (Matt. 5:3). About this virtue, and its importance, I was relatively ignorant.

Humility should be the aim of the spiritual disciplines. You can witness, serve, study your Bible, and pray, and not grow in this virtue. In fact, these disciplines can inadvertently have the opposite effect. They can actually amplify your pride. The Pharisees were exceedingly disciplined, yet pride in their discipline was their primary characteristic, and that is why God opposed them. The Bible repeatedly warns, "God opposes the proud, but gives grace to the humble" (James 4:6, quoting Prov. 3:34). God opposed the Pharisees by hiding himself from them; and he graces the humble by drawing them into a deeper experience of their relationship with himself. "He regards the lowly, but the haughty he knows from afar" (Ps. 138:6). Spiritual disciplines are an important means of grace. We should practice them. But if they are making you proud, they might be counterproductive; in fact, they might be a stumbling block—a wedge between you and God.

Why is humility the indispensable virtue? You can't get close to God without it. You can't love God or man without it. You can't obey without it. You can't become anything that God wants you to be without it. "This [humility] is a great and most essential thing in true religion," wrote Jonathan Edwards. "The whole frame of the gospel, everything appertaining to the new covenant, and all God's dispensations towards fallen man, *are calculated to bring to pass this effect.*"[3]

If this is true, and it is, replicating humility should be the fundamental goal of our ministry. Whether preaching, counseling, or witnessing, our goal should be a growing faith rooted in the rich compost of humility.

HUMILITY AND *PRIDE* DEFINED

Humility is one of the least understood spiritual fruits. It is not self-hatred or lack of self-confidence. Humility and low self-image are not the same thing. Indeed, they are polar opposites. Increasing humility brings rest with self, with God, and with life's circumstances. It produces real lasting joy and healthy self-image. Humility is the ability to see spiritual reality, to see things as they really are. *It is the capacity to see myself in God's light, in the context of his holiness and my sinfulness.* In other words, it is the ability to see self, and this world, through God's eyes. God empowers the humble person to increasingly see himself as he really is: "wretched, pitiable, poor, blind, and naked" (Rev. 3:17). The person growing in humility sees his gifts and faults, his strengths and weaknesses, with increasing clarity. Ironically, as we will see, this humility lays the sure foundation for real contentment and healthy self-image because the humble Christian also increasingly sees and *feels* God's great personal love. The truly humble believer has a low view of himself, but an increasingly high view of God and his fellow man.

Pride is the opposite. It is spiritual blindness. It is a delusional, inflated view of self. It is unreality on steroids. And the scary part is this: The thing to which we are most blind is our pride. A demonic Catch-22, pride causes us to chase our spiritual tails. We cannot see pride—even though it is our most grievous, disabling sin—because its very nature is blindness, and the first thing to which it is blind is its own existence. Even though God was speaking to me about my arrogance through Isaiah 66:2 and 1 Corinthians 13:12, because pride blinded me I could not see it. Dazzled by my own self-respect, I could not see my failings. Pride is a spiritual veil blinding us to the truth about ourselves and God. The proud person has a high view of self but a low view of God and his brother.

"There is no fault which we are more *unconscious* of in ourselves," wrote C. S. Lewis. "If you think you are not conceited, it means you are very conceited indeed."[4]

Here is the great paradox: the proud man thinks he is humble, but the humble man thinks he is proud. The humble man sees his arrogance. He sees it clearly, and as a result he aggressively pursues a life of humility, but he doesn't think of himself as humble. The proud man is completely unaware of his pride. Of all men he is most convinced that he is humble.

WHERE PRIDE AND HUMILITY TAKE US

Notice that Isaiah 66:2 reads, "This is the one to whom I will look: he who is humble and contrite in spirit and trembles at my word." There is an important progression in this text.

Humility always blossoms into something more beautiful. It is the root that feeds the other spiritual fruits. In this verse it leads to real contrition, which then deepens into trembling at God's Word. In other words, humility sensitizes us to God's Word, motivating and equipping us to hear God's voice. (See below.) Humility provoked Paul to write: "work out your own salvation with fear and *trembling*" (Phil. 2:12). It motivated David to "rejoice with *trembling*" (Ps. 2:11). Humility enhances our love for God's Word and our dependence on God's Word. The humble joyfully tremble at God's Word, eager to obey, seeking God's encouragement and correction.

Humility → Contrition → Trembling

Pride, on the other hand, metamorphoses into something more dreadful. It is the fountainhead of evil. Instead of contrition, pride morphs into self-righteousness, and instead of trembling at God's Word, self-righteousness terminates in *despising* God's Word, or at best apathy.[5] (See below.) This can happen to well-intentioned Christians—even men like David. When Nathan confronted David about his sin with Bathsheba, the prophet accused David of "*despis[ing]* the word of the LORD" (2 Sam. 12:9). To God, the conviction that we are above his threats is the sin of despising him. David must have thought, *I can commit adultery and get away with it. After all, I'm the man after God's own heart.* But no one "trembles" at God's Word and disobeys God, as David did. In other words, we sin because we are proud, and God sees our pride as the sin of despising him. A proud man cannot tremble at God's Word.

Pride → Self Righteousness → Despising God's Word

Not so the humble man, the one who trembles at God's Word. He takes God's Word seriously. He believes its promises

26

and threats, and he trembles. He fears God. He loves God. He needs God. He abides in the love of God. God's Word is a heart-piercing arrow, and he loves its convicting, piercing work. He knows what he deserves, and every day he revels in the amazing grace of God that has sheltered him from the terrors of God's justice.

Since humility ends in trembling at God's Word, it brings us into real communion with God. It sensitizes us to God's voice. It opens our ears to his instructions. It amplifies gratitude. It intensifies dependence. In other words, the humble see their need for God. That is why the Bible tells us:

- God *esteems* the humble (Isa. 66:2).
- He *dwells* with the "contrite and lowly" (Isa. 57:15).
- He *blesses* the poor in spirit (Matt. 5:3).
- He *graces* the humble (James 4:6).
- He *guides* and *teaches* the humble (Ps. 25:9).
- He *regards* the lowly (Ps. 138:6).

Because we are blind to our pride, it is always a problem. But there is a sense in which it is especially pernicious today. Humility has almost disappeared from our spiritual lexicon. "What has changed," notes Cornelius Plantinga, "is that, in much of contemporary American culture, aggressive self-regard is no longer viewed with alarm. Instead people praise and promote it."[6]

Self-esteem, self-promotion, self-congratulation, and self-admiration are now celebrated as virtues. Western culture has evangelized the church. But God calls his people to be different, to separate themselves from the values of this fallen world.

So far, we have noted that humility is necessary for both intimacy with God and spiritual fruitfulness. We have defined *humility*. We have noted where both pride and humility take us. The remainder of this chapter will make four observations to attempt to convince you that humility matters:

- First, humility is necessary for conversion.
- Second, humility is necessary for sanctification.
- Third, we need humility to see what God is doing.
- Fourth, the gospel demonstrates humility and produces a faith that culminates in growing humility.

HUMILITY PRECEDES CONVERSION

God saves those who believe, not those who work. But the belief that saves always produces some level of humbling. The bad news humbles us and prepares us for the good news. By *bad news* I mean the doctrines of God's wrath, the final judgment, and the sinfulness of man.

The bad news is conspicuously absent from the modern church. Millions attend Christian churches with a "faith" that has produced little or no humbling. For example, multitudes of regular churchgoers have never been taught the doctrine of sin. According to George Barna, over 70 percent of professing Christians in North America don't understand, or believe in, original sin. They believe that men and women are basically good.[7] But true faith, the faith that saves, teaches us about sin. It always humbles. If there is no humbling, it is unlikely that saving faith has occurred.

Augustine (354–430) popularized this insight. He suggested that humility is the soil from which all the virtues grow and pride the soil that produces the vices. Until the Reformation, this view was generally accepted. Then John Calvin (1509–64), who was a student and fan of Augustine, suggested a deeper analysis. Just as unbelief is the source of pride, faith is the beginning and source of humility. Think about it. Real, heartfelt faith in the gospel always humbles. After all, it is a message about man in sin, under judgment, standing before an angry God, but a God who wants to be our friend. Our predicament is bad. We cannot improve it with human effort. God is the only One who can solve our problem, and God commands us to respond—but not by "trying harder." Instead, we are to abandon all confidence in human effort. We are to merely believe, repent, and live by *unmerited* favor. No matter how you slice it, this is humbling. By contrast, unbelief says, "I am good enough. Surely, if God exists, he will accept me. After all, I am every bit as good as my neighbor." These attitudes are fruits of arrogance.

In other words, biblical faith always initiates a humbling process. By contrast, unbelief promotes arrogance. You can profess belief in an orthodox creed and lack this humbling faith. If humility is this important, it stands to reason that God has designed the gospel to produce the kind of faith that humbles men and women, that brings them face-to-face with their moral and spiritual bankruptcy, that confronts them with God's gracious solution.

That is the argument of this book. I hope to convince you, and in the process change the way you conduct ministry.

This humbling occurs when we assent to certain vital truths. For example, justification is by faith alone. This doctrine assumes that I am hopelessly lost, that my moral condition is desperate, and that my best efforts will avail me nothing. I am a sinner and cannot save myself. My only hope is God's mercy. I enter into it by believing, not working. This is humbling.

Saving faith also confesses that I am not smart enough to make my own rules. It believes that God knows best what is right and wrong. It concurs with the Bible about who God is, the sinfulness of sin, God's sovereignty in creation and salvation, the nature of Jesus Christ, and a host of other issues. Saving faith confesses that hell is real, that I am in deep trouble with God, and that I will end up in hell unless I put my trust in Christ's sinless life and substitutionary death. Saving faith confesses that Christ is Lord and decides to obey him. Each confession makes us smaller and Christ larger.

Therefore, we should not be surprised when Scripture reads: "You *save* a humble people" (Ps. 18:27); "The LORD . . . *adorns* the humble with salvation" (Ps. 149:4); "Blessed are the poor in spirit, for *theirs is the kingdom* of heaven" (Matt. 5:3). In the Matthew verse, "poor in spirit" is a synonym for humility. Later Jesus said, "Truly, I say to you, unless you turn and become like children, you will never *enter* the kingdom of heaven" (Matt. 18:3). Becoming childlike implies simplicity, dependence, and above all humility. Each of these texts implies one thing: humility is a prerequisite for conversion. Scripture does not say that we are saved by humility. We are saved by faith alone. These texts want us to know that the faith that saves immediately begins the humbling process. If that is the case, we should seek to communicate a message that humbles. To do this, our gospel must begin with the bad news *before* it progresses to the good news.

None of this should surprise us. If the great sin is pride, God must have designed the mechanics of conversion to produce its opposite: humility. Jonathan Edwards notes that humility "is a great and most essential thing in true religion." Then he says, "*The whole frame of the gospel, and everything appertaining to the new covenant, and all God's dispensations towards fallen man, are calculated to bring to pass this effect [humility] in the hearts of men*. They that are destitute of this, have no true religion, whatever profession they may make, and how high soever their religious affections may be."[8]

The Pharisees were Jesus' enemies. They resisted him at every turn. Why? They were proud, and their pride barred them from salvation. They refused to do what those who get saved do. They refused to humble themselves. With this in mind, Jesus said, "Those who are well have no need of a physician, but those who are sick. I came not to call the righteous, but sinners" (Mark 2:17). For the Pharisee, salvation meant renouncing confidence in his righteousness. It meant admitting that despite his formidable self-discipline, he is "sick." This they were unwilling to do.

The Pharisees were the neediest people in Israel. They were sinners under the wrath of God, hurtling headlong toward final judgment, yet they refused to humble themselves and believe. Why? They were convinced of their goodness. They thought they could merit God's favor. It is no different today. The default condition of every unbeliever is Pharisee to the core.

If this is true, we should seek to humble those to whom we communicate the gospel. In later chapters, we will see that this is exactly what God has designed the gospel to do. We will also discuss ways to help those to whom we minister humble themselves so that they can be converted.

HUMILITY PRECEDES SANCTIFICATION

Humility also matters because it is necessary for sanctification. *Sanctification* is the theological term for the process of growth in godliness that occurs over time in all true believers. I grow asparagus in my garden. Asparagus thrive on steer manure. Last year I failed to fertilize them. The crop was sparse and short-lived. Humility is the same. All the fruits of the Spirit feed on it. It is the necessary fertilizer that nourishes love, joy, peace, patience, kindness, goodness, faithfulness, gentleness, and self-control.

After the first beatitude, "Blessed are the poor in spirit," seven more follow—mourning for sin, meekness, hungering for righteousness, the capacity to be merciful, purity of heart, peacemaking, and the willingness to be persecuted for righteousness' sake. They all have this in common: they require

31

poverty of spirit, the idea conveyed by the first beatitude. In other words, they require humility.

The first three spiritual fruits mentioned in Galatians 5—love, joy, and peace—make a good case study. To love someone else, you must humble yourself and "count [the other person] more significant than" yourself (Phil. 2:3). The lower Paul went in his own eyes, the higher others arose, and the greater his capacity to love them. "For Christ's love compels us," he confessed to the Corinthians (2 Cor. 5:14 NIV). How did it compel Paul? It compelled him to make the most stupendous love sacrifices ever recorded this side of Christ's cross. He did this because the needs of others were more important than his own. This is what it means to be humble. It does not mean a bad opinion of self relative to others. It means not thinking about yourself at all. It means making others more significant than yourself by focusing entirely on their needs and wants (see Phil. 2:3–5).

Humility is also the fertilizer that feeds joy. It is no accident that the great passage on humility—Philippians 2:5–8—is contained in the letter that mentions joy more frequently than any other book of the Bible. What is the connection? Humble people are happy people. They have no secret ambition to be somebody. They are at rest. They serve a big God, and that also is a source of joy. The knowledge of God's love (a love revealed increasingly to the humble) is another source of joy. The love for God that follows humility also inspires joy. Finally, they "overflow with thanksgiving" (Col. 2:7 NLT). Why? They know what they deserve: eternal judgment. No matter how bad life gets, they are never getting what they really deserve, and for this reason they abound with gratitude.

Humility produces peace. Personal peace with God, man, and circumstances is a fruit of humility. "We have peace with God through our Lord Jesus Christ" (Rom. 5:1). This means, assuming that we have repented of sin, that our peace with God does not rise and fall on our performance. It rises and falls on Christ's performance provided by God the Father for our salvation. Failure to do our devotions does not disturb our peace with God. Assuming that we have repented, failure to perform our parenting or marital duties does not disturb our peace with God. In the same way, a bout of impulsive spending cannot disturb our peace with God. Why? Such peace doesn't depend on our righteousness. That peace depends on Christ's righteousness imputed to us. It takes growing humility to accept this fact. Pride is the root of all performance-based acceptance. Humility is required for "the peace that surpasses understanding" that Paul said would "guard your hearts and your minds in Christ Jesus" (Phil. 4:7). Like Paul, humble people are intensely aware of their sin, but because they are humble, they are even more aware of God's mercy and grace. That is why they enjoy peace with God and man. Ultimately, they know that nothing depends on them.

In the same way, humility precedes the other fruits— patience, kindness, goodness, faithfulness, gentleness, and self-control. This is a second reason why we should pursue humility. And it is why Jesus began the Sermon on the Mount with an exhortation to display poverty of spirit.

HUMILITY EQUIPS US TO SEE WHAT GOD IS DOING

There is a third reason that humility matters. Spiritual pride hardens us to what God is doing, while humility does just the opposite. It opens our eyes to what God is doing. Since whatever God is doing is always humbling, and since religious pride hates to be humbled, religious pride always resists God's activity even while it thinks it is serving God.

Jesus was able to work with adulterers, thieves, and criminals, but the Pharisees were his implacable enemies. They could not see God at work in Christ, and religious pride was their defining sin. Religious pride hates what God is doing. It has no capacity to discern what God is doing. It has no capacity to enter into what God is doing. It lacks the ability to join God in what he is doing. Instead, it aggressively resists and persecutes God's work.

Jesus tried to humble the Pharisees. How did they respond? They crucified him and thought they were doing God a favor. Each of us is capable of doing the same.

That is why Scripture says, "The LORD detests all the proud of heart" (Prov. 16:5 NIV); "I hate pride and arrogance" (Prov. 8:13 NIV). *Hate* is a strong word. Yet God hates pride. He hates it because it aggressively resists his agenda.

Religious pride has many discernible symptoms. Critical speech is one. The feeling of spiritual elitism is another. After my conversion I joined a vibrant, growing church. We believed that we were on the inside track. We were working where God was working. We began to feel sorry for the other churches that weren't as discerning as we were. I couldn't see why every Christian didn't join our church. *If the other churches were really listening to God,* I reasoned, *they would do what we are doing.* This is how spiritual pride thinks. It is ugly, and God always resists it.

Spiritual pride is the great temptation of religious people. The Holy Spirit converts us; then the devil attempts to morph the good that God has done into this anti-God state of mind. Spiritual pride deafened the Pharisees to Jesus' words and work. It has been this way throughout history. Religion is always the first institution to persecute and resist whatever God's Spirit is doing. It must. Pride is blindness. And religious pride is always blind to what the Holy Spirit is doing.

Here is the bottom line. Since God's activity always humbles, and since spiritual pride hates to be humbled, it resists God's work. As we have seen, the Pharisees crucified Jesus. The Jews persecuted Paul. To the degree that spiritual pride permeates our lives, we will also resist the work of the Holy Spirit. By contrast, humility frees us to join God in his work.

THE GOSPEL IS A DISPLAY OF HUMILITY

The fourth and last reason humility is so important is that the gospel is a display of humility. If the root of evil is pride, and if the main virtue needed is humility, then we would expect Jesus' life and death to be a pride-conquering display of soul-abasing humility. And that is what we find. This is how the second chapter of Philippians describes the gospel. Jesus washed away our filthy pride with the cleansing power of divine humility.

> Have this mind among yourselves, which is yours in Christ Jesus, who, though he was in the form of God, did not count equality with God a thing to be grasped, but made himself nothing, taking the form of a servant [slave], being born in the likeness of men. And being found in human form, he humbled himself by becoming obedient to the point of death, even death on a cross. (Phil. 2:5–8)

In seventy short English words Paul sums up the life of Christ, and what he describes is a galactic *descent* of infinite dimensions. I say "infinite" purposefully. By definition, the distance between anything infinite and anything finite is infinite. The distance never lessens. You never arrive at something infinite. It stretches out forever. Christ's status before becoming man was "infinite." His post-birth human status was finite. Therefore, his incarnation was an infinite descent. It cannot be measured. John Flavel (1627–91), one of the English Puritan preachers, summed it up this way:

> For the sun to fall from its sphere, and be degraded into a wandering atom; for an angel to be turned out of heaven, and be converted into a silly fly or worm, had been no such great abasement; for they were but creatures before, and so they would abide still, though in an inferior order or

35

species of creatures. The distance betwixt the highest and lowest species of creatures, is but a finite distance. The angel and the worm dwell not so far apart. But for the infinite glorious Creator of all things, to become a creature, is a mystery exceeding all human understanding. The distance between God and the highest order of creatures, is an infinite distance.[9]

God is infinitely just, and his law must be satisfied. "Everyone who exalts himself will be humbled," Jesus warned, "and he who humbles himself will be exalted" (Luke 14:11). It is an immutable spiritual principle. God has engraved it into the very fabric of creation. No creature can be exalted to heavenly reward until it has first thoroughly humbled itself with obedience. We have a major problem. We have all exalted ourselves in disobedience.

That is why Christ descended an infinite distance and became flesh—to satisfy God's justice for proud sinners like you and me. When we believe, God unites us with Christ in his descent, which culminated in the cross. When God exalted Christ through his resurrection and ascension, we were exalted with him. Christ's humiliation makes our exaltation possible.

Notice: If it took an infinite descent to atone for our pride, then it follows that our pride must be infinitely offensive to God. It also follows that unforgiven pride must receive an infinite punishment. That is why hell is eternal. It never ends. The offense is so great that a suffering of infinite duration cannot satisfy God's justice and qualify the sinner for heavenly reward.

Christ's incarnation is the measure of God's hatred of pride. It is also the measure of his infinite love for proud, undeserving people like you and me. Only an infinite descent can adequately express God's love, a love that Paul said "surpasses knowledge" (Eph. 3:19).

WHERE THIS BOOK IS GOING

I hope this chapter has convinced you of the importance of humility. Without it, there is no salvation or sanctification. Instead, there is violent hatred and persecution of all that God's Spirit is doing. The gospel is a display of heavenly humility.

If humility is this important, then every aspect of Christian ministry should be a humbling ministry. We should pursue humility in our personal lives, and we should engineer Christian ministry to produce it in those we love. "Ministry" applies to parents, Christians attempting to evangelize their friends, pastors, Christian counselors, Bible study leaders, Sunday school teachers, local church elders, and others. All should communicate a gospel that humbles those they serve.

Because we are a proud culture, it is hard for us to see the extent of our problem. Chapter 2 will attempt to convince us that pride is our cultural sin. It will use the social sciences, great Christian leaders of past centuries, and biblical testimony to make this point.

CONCLUSION

I was a Christian twenty-two years before I began to understand my personal arrogance. The understanding started on Oregon's coastal highway in the fall of 1993, and it was all God's gracious, undeserved gift. God let me see my pride as he saw it, and everything changed.

We have seen that humility is not a negative view of self. Rather, it is the God-given ability to see self and God as we really are. Humility is the key to intimacy with God. It is the doorway to personal happiness.

We have also learned that humility and pride have consequences. Humility produces contrition, which causes us to

37

tremble at God's Word. Pride produces self-righteousness, which leads to despising or rejecting God's Word.

Although there are many reasons why humility matters, this chapter focused on four. First, it is necessary for conversion. Second, it is necessary for sanctification. Third, it enables us to see what God is doing. Fourth, this subject is so important that God sent his Son to put on a massive display of humility and save us through it.

We have noted that pride is blindness. It follows that a proud culture will be least able to see that it has a problem with pride. We are a proud culture. The point of the next chapter is to convince us of the extent and magnitude of our arrogance.

2

Convincing the Patient

There are those who are clean in their own eyes,
  but are not washed from their filth. (Prov. 30:12)

In her heart she says,
  "I sit as a queen;
I am no widow,
  and mourning I shall never see." (Rev. 18:7)

DON MADE AN APPOINTMENT with his family physician for a routine exam. He was in his late fifties and felt good. After much probing, checking, and thumping, the physician took a blood draw and sent his patient home. A few days later the doctor called. "Your PSA is elevated. I am concerned. I want to do more tests."

Another week passed. "I have bad news," the doctor reluctantly reported. "You have prostate cancer, and it is in an advanced state. We need to operate soon. But I need to warn you: there is a significant chance that the surgery will make you impotent."

Don was shocked. He felt fine. There was no pain, no loss of energy, no soreness. He felt no different than he had the day before the physical. Whom should he believe? Was he really sick? Did he really have cancer? If the doctor was right, and he hesitated, he might die. On the other hand, surgery might end in impotence. What if it did and his tumor was not really malignant? How could he really know? Ultimately, he would have to trust the physician's diagnosis.

The spiritual life works the same way. God's Word gives us a thorough diagnosis of our spiritual condition. Pride, however, smothers us in a false sense of security. Whom should we believe? Is the human condition as bad as the Bible suggests?

The purpose of this chapter is to convince you that chapter 1 was right. No matter how we feel about ourselves, pride is our problem. It alienates us from God.

As we saw in chapter 1, the first symptom of our corporate pride is our blindness to it. We are like Don. We have a disease that we don't see or feel. We must take it by faith. Yet as we do, as we humble self, the symptoms of our pride become increasingly apparent. They are all around us. This was my experience.

When I was twenty-five, I first read C. S. Lewis's *Mere Christianity*. One of the chapters was "The Great Sin." It was about pride, and it was all new to me. I remember reading the last sentence in the chapter, "If you think you are not conceited, it means you are very conceited indeed,"[1] and thinking, *I don't feel conceited. In fact, I feel humble, but I have a feeling that this is true. It has the ring of authenticity. I wish I could see its application to me.* Thirty-five years later I read the same chapter and thought to myself, *How could I have been so blind? How could I not see my arrogance? Now, I see pride lurking behind every thought, attitude, desire, and action.* What had changed? I had asked God for humility. As God humbled me, the symptoms of my pride became increasingly obvious. They were all around me.

40

The bottom line is this: too much self-esteem, not low self-esteem, is our basic cultural problem. When, in later chapters, we discuss how to help others grow in humility, confidence in the content of this chapter will be important.

Most of us are like Don. We have a diagnosis that we don't feel. The aim of this chapter is to help us feel and see the problem.

First, we will examine the problem. Then we will explore evidence from the social sciences and the Bible that confirms the diagnosis. Because we are blind to our cultural sins and excesses, we will query the great saints of history, men outside our culture, for a diagnosis of our situation.

THE PROBLEM

Most American Christians assume a low view of God and a high view of self. It is part of our cultural milieu, and that is what makes it so deadly. "We may be sure that the characteristic blindness of the twentieth century," wrote C. S. Lewis in another essay, "—the blindness about which posterity will ask, 'But how *could* they have thought that?'—lies where we have never suspected it."[2] Lewis was right. It is easy for us to see the errors of the past. The eleventh-century Christian assumed the legitimacy of the Crusades. He believed that God wanted European Christians to conquer the Holy Lands. In the same way, the eighteenth-century New England Puritan assumed the legitimacy of slavery. We look back on their assumptions with 20/20 clarity. *How could they have been so blind?*

Yet it is not just past generations that are blind where least suspected. We are also blind where we least expect it. We assume the rightfulness of attitudes that future generations will view with abhorrence. I believe our high view of self falls into that category.

According to Ray Ortlund Jr., "America is a self-ocracy, *and the church is little different.* . . . We are more American than we think we are, less Christian than we think we are, and all too content with what we are." Ortlund concludes, "Self-absorption is the mark of our age."[3] He hit the nail on the head. Our culture is preoccupied with self, in love with self, concerned about self, and constantly massaging self. Our culture assumes that selfish individualism is a virtue. What makes it so deadly is that we assume it, and what we assume we don't see. What we assume we tend to embrace uncritically.

This assumption shows up in our advertising. No one knows America like those who market to it. Advertisers get paid to find America's hot button and push it. What really makes us tick? What do we really value? What drives us? When all is said and done, the button is this self-centeredness. Although the cross reminds us that we deserve crucifixion, McDonald's tells us that we "deserve a break today." Although Peter tells us to *abstain* from the lusts of the flesh, Nike urges us to "just do it!" And although the Bible tells us that God makes the rules, and that on the day of judgment we will give an accounting for breaking those rules, Outback Steakhouse says, "No rules, just right." One of my favorites I found on the back of a bottle of Smartwater: "Play first. You can make up the rules later."

Most disturbingly, our culture assumes that this self-orientation is healthy, in fact necessary for personal well-being. By contrast, previous generations (even unbelievers) thought it positively destructive. *Self* magazine would have been an embarrassment in the 1950s. It bothers few today. My contention is that this same fog of cultural hubris (another word for *pride*) has engulfed the church. It blinds us to the absence of, or need for, humility.

If it is for the right reasons, healthy self-image can be virtuous. Modern culture, however, exhorts us to grow in self-esteem—but for all the wrong reasons. It exhorts us to feel good because we are good, to feel worthy and loved because we are lovable. "We are wonderful," we are told, whether we do anything to merit love or not.

Although the concept of self-image is not in the Bible, a parallel idea—peace with God—is. "Since we have been justified by faith, we have peace with God" (Rom. 5:1). But this peace, or well-being, has a completely different *basis* from the modern drive for self-esteem. Christians feel good about themselves not because they are wonderful, but because *God* is wonderful. Although we are wonderfully made in God's image, we are fallen. We are sinners, fatally flawed at the deepest level. God's wrath rests on us. We are at war with him. Any peace with God is a gift from God to unworthy sinners. So the source of our peace does not lie in us. It lies with God.

So what is the basis for a Christian's self-image? It is simple. God loves us even in our fallen condition. God does not love us because we are good but despite the fact that we are not. This shifts the focus from self to God. It shifts our confidence from self to God. In our unredeemed state, we are God's enemies. Even so, God loves us. He loves creatures that deserve to be hated. If you are a Christian, you are eternally secure in that love. And you are loved because of grace, not works (Rom. 8:35–39).

The secular *basis* for self-image is personal performance. I feel good about myself because I am good. This assumption has invaded the church. It has distorted the Christian worldview. To the degree that we embrace it, the priority of humility will be obscured.

We see and feel the contrast when we read Christians from previous centuries. They assumed the opposite. A quick reading of *The Valley of Vision*, a collection of seventeenth-century Puritan prayers, is a good example. These prayers are saturated in confessions of sin, the unworthiness of the person praying, and his smallness. To twenty-first-century readers, Puritans' prayers seem negative and depressing. These men assume that they deserve God's judgment, and they are amazed by God's grace.

By contrast, most moderns assume God's love. They assume that they *deserve* to be loved by God. They maintain high opinions of self. With the exception of Joseph Stalin or Adolf Hitler, we cannot imagine God judging anyone. It seems so unfair. We are good people. God's judgments are too harsh. So we don't talk about hell. It is embarrassing. How could a loving God send "good people, sincere people" to hell? "It is perplexing how little has been written on pride in recent years," notes Dr. Stuart Scott. "To read very much on the subject of pride, one must read Puritan literature."[4] The absence of writing on pride and humility is one of the first signs that secular culture has evangelized the church, not vice versa.

Western culture assumes that we are already humble, that self-hatred is our basic problem. The Bible contends that we are proud, and that the inflated self is our fundamental problem.

Who is right? Is our problem too much self-hatred or too much self-love? To answer that question, the remainder of this chapter will examine the findings of social psychology, the testimony of the Bible, and the comments of Christians from previous generations.

SOCIAL PSYCHOLOGY SPEAKS

Social psychology is the study of individual people's behavior as it affects, and is affected by, the behavior of groups around them. Social psychologists have conducted many experiments on the subject of self-esteem. Their studies consistently show that the average person takes credit for his virtues, feels superior to societal norms, and blames his environment for his failings. Social psychology confirms that the average person, when comparing self with social norms, has high self-esteem.

For example, we justify ourselves: "I am selfish because my parents didn't love me." But we congratulate *ourselves* for our patience or our athletic ability. People say, "I abuse my children because I didn't receive the proper training from my parents." Then the same people take full credit for their children's academic achievements. Pride urges us to take credit for good behavior but blame our environment for our failings: "The serpent deceived me, and I ate" (Gen. 3:13). We are all good children of Eve. "Simply put," notes Dr. David Myers, "people see their failings as normal and their virtues as rare. . . . To paraphrase Elizabeth Barrett Browning, 'How do I love me? Let me count the ways.' "[5]

Experiments show that most people see themselves more positively than their friends and relatives do. Most Americans believe that they are more ethical than average, less prejudiced than average, and healthier than average.[6]

For example: "In one College Entrance Examination Board survey of 829,000 high school seniors, 0 percent (that is not a typo) rated themselves below average in the subjective and valued 'ability to get along with others,' 60 percent rated themselves in the top 10 percent, and 25 percent saw themselves among the top 1 percent."[7]

Nine in ten managers rate themselves superior to their peers. Another survey, taken of people in Australia, reports that nearly nine in ten rate their job performance higher than that of their peers. In three surveys, nine in ten college professors rated themselves superior to their colleagues. And most drivers—even those recently hospitalized after a driving accident—believe themselves safer and more skilled than the average driver.[8] "The one thing that unites all human beings, regardless of age, gender, religion, economic status or ethnic background," observes the humorist Dave Barry, "is that deep down inside, we all believe that we are above average drivers."[9]

Attempting to personally verify these studies, I queried sixty adults who attended a Bible study I taught. I asked them to rate themselves average, above average, or below average on certain moral and nonmoral qualities.

The results? Ninety-eight percent said that they were average or above-average drivers. Ninety percent said that they served more than average. Ninety-eight percent said that their ability to get along with others was average or above average. Ninety-six percent felt that their parenting skills were average or above average. Eighty-three percent felt that their level of compassion was average or above average. The odds suggest that 50 percent of my class were average or below average, yet virtually no one rated himself or herself below average in any category. What makes this most amazing is that these respondents had been exposed to Bible teaching about sin for several years.

Conclusion? Self-esteem is alive and well in the church.

Truth be known, most of us are like the Russian novelist Leo Tolstoy. In his book *Intellectuals*, Paul Johnson notes that Tolstoy was a moral monster. Yet at age twenty-five, he wrote in his diary:

> Read a work on the literary characterization of genius today, and this awoke in me the conviction that I am a remarkable man both as regards capacity and eagerness to work. I have not yet met a single man who was morally as good as I, and believe that I do not remember an instance in my life when I was not attracted to what is good and was not ready to sacrifice anything to it.[10]

Cornelius Plantinga, citing an ad in the "Strictly Personal" section of *New York* magazine, summarizes the spirit of our age:

> **Strikingly Beautiful**—Ivy League graduate. Playful, passionate, perceptive, elegant, bright, articulate, original in mind,

unique in spirit. I possess a rare balance of beauty and depth, sophistication and earthiness, seriousness and a love of fun.[11]

In a survey by *U.S. News & World Report*, Americans were asked who they thought was most likely to go to heaven. Sixty-five percent thought Oprah Winfrey and Michael Jordan were "very likely" to go to heaven. Seventy-nine percent believed Mother Teresa would go to heaven.

Only one person scored higher than Mother Teresa. You guessed it—the respondent. Over 80 percent taking the survey felt it "very likely" that they would go to heaven.[12] We not only feel better than society's norms, but also feel confident that we can earn God's favor through our sincerity or our best efforts.

Sometimes people do feel inferior to their peers. But it tends to be in the presence of a superior *individual* rather than cultural norms—one who is better-looking, smarter, better-educated, or more wealthy. But when comparing ourselves with the norms of society, most of us feel above average. In fact, overconfidence is so prominent in social research that many secular social scientists have concluded that evolution has built a significant load of arrogance into us for survival. The experiments of social scientists confirm what the Bible has taught for four thousand years: arrogance is our basic problem.[13] "Contrary to the presumption that most people suffer from low self-esteem, or feelings of inferiority," notes Dr. Myers, "researchers consistently find that most people exhibit a *self-serving bias.*"[14]

Please note: I am not saying that guilt is not a pervasive problem. It is. What I am saying is that pride is an even greater problem. Moreover, pride—too high an opinion of self—rather than low self-image is the root that energizes most guilt. "That's the paradox of self-esteem," notes Edward Welch. "Low self-esteem usually means that I think too highly of myself. I'm too self-involved, I feel I deserve better than what I have. The reason I feel bad about myself is that I aspire to something more. I want just a few minutes of greatness. I am a peasant who wants to be king. . . . This is the dark quieter side of pride—thwarted pride."[15]

All of this matters because pride stands in opposition to the humility necessary for conversion, sanctification, and the ability to please God.

THE BIBLE SPEAKS

What does the Bible have to say about all this? First, it is important to note that there are no verses exhorting us to build up our self-image. Many verses speak of God's great love and exhort us to live in that love. But because the Bible does not assume that low self-image is our problem, it never asks us to improve our self-image or to think higher of ourselves. In fact, it assumes just the opposite.

God assumes what the social research confirms: that our basic problem is arrogance—self-deception at the deepest level about who we really are. Because of this, his Word commands us to humble ourselves before the Lord (James 4:10). He warns us to "clothe [our]selves . . . with humility toward one another, for God opposes the proud but gives grace to the humble" (1 Peter 5:5). His Spirit exhorts us not to think of ourselves "more highly than [we] ought, but rather . . . with sober judgment" (Rom. 12:3 NIV).

God knows that we are conceited, so he commands us to "not be proud, but be willing to associate with people of low position," and to "not be conceited" (Rom. 12:16 NIV). Because we naturally consider ourselves more important than others, God exhorts us to "do nothing from rivalry or conceit, but in humility count others more significant than yourselves" (Phil. 2:3).

48

The Bible constantly exhorts us to *feel good about God*, and to acquire good feelings about self by looking at God rather than self. But we have turned the tables. We have absorbed the lies of humanistic, therapeutic psychology. We want to feel good about self not because God loves us and died for us despite our sinful condition, but because we are inherently good and deserving.

According to Edward Welch, "the good news of Jesus is *not* intended to make us feel good about ourselves. Instead, the good news humbles us."[16] This humbling is necessary for a healthy self-image. We will see how this seemingly small difference in emphasis widens into a gaping crevasse in practice. For one on the wrong side of the gap, it means diminished Christian experience and usefulness.

Not only does the Bible stress the need for humility, but as we saw in chapter 1, it promises infinite spiritual riches to the one who finds it.

JOB, ISAIAH, AND PETER SPEAK OUT

Listen to some of the great Bible heroes on this subject. They remind us that we grow in humility by looking outward to God, not inward to self.

Job was a paragon of virtue. He had less to feel sinful about than 99 percent of those reading this page. The Bible goes to great lengths to remind us that he was "blameless and upright; he feared God and shunned evil" (Job 1:1 NIV). But when, after his immense suffering, God appeared to him, how did Job respond? He said, "I *despise myself*, and repent in dust and ashes" (Job 42:5–6). The King James Version reads "abhor myself." And it was only after Job despised himself that God restored his material wealth sevenfold. Job learned to despise himself by looking at God, not himself.

Like Job, the prophet Isaiah was a virtuous man. While Isaiah was worshiping in Solomon's temple, the Lord appeared to him high and lifted up, with his train filling the temple. Mighty six-winged seraphim hovered above, thundering, "Holy, holy, holy is the LORD of hosts; the whole earth is full of his glory!" (Isa. 6:3). The train of God's robe filled the temple. The building shook. Smoke was everywhere. How did Isaiah respond—with self-esteem or God-esteem?

In agony of spirit, Isaiah cried: "Woe is me! For I am lost; for I am a man of unclean lips, and I dwell in the midst of a people of unclean lips; for my eyes have seen the King, the LORD of hosts!" (Isa. 6:5). In the presence of God's holy-white purity, all Isaiah could see was the putrid nature of his speech—how it proceeded from a defiled, deceitful, and wicked heart (Jer. 17:9; Matt. 12:34). As he had done with Job, God began to use Isaiah only after this humbling. And like Job, Isaiah saw himself by looking at God, not himself.

This phenomenon occurred again when Jesus miraculously filled Simon's nets to overflowing. Peter, by nature an impulsive, confident man, saw himself through the lens of reality for the first time. He turned his face from Jesus and said, "Depart from me, for I am a sinful man, O Lord" (Luke 5:8). This statement marked the beginning of Peter's service. "Do not be afraid," Jesus told him. "From now on you will be catching men" (v. 10). Peter pulled his boat ashore, left everything, and followed Jesus. What Peter didn't know was that his descent into humility was just beginning. He would need to go even lower in his own eyes (he would need to deny Jesus three times) before God could use him.

Later, Jesus took Peter, James, and John up the mountain to pray. Jesus unveiled his glory, allowing the three to see him in his preincarnate majesty. His face became like the sun shining in full strength. His garments shone with an incandescent whiteness. He was the *shekinah* glory that indwelt the Old Testament tabernacle. What was his disciples' response? "They fell on their faces and were *terrified*" (Matt. 17:6). In God's light they saw themselves accurately, and all confidence in personal virtue evaporated.

"CLASSIC" CHRISTIANS SPEAK OUT

Many fathers of the faith have also addressed this subject. Humility was their priority. Not surprisingly, their comments swim against the current of our age.

Unlike modern Christians, our spiritual ancestors assumed that too much self-esteem (too much pride or hubris) was man's essential problem. The great saints of past centuries held a low view of man and a high view of God. Most historical orthodox Christian writing shares this assumption. These men assumed that humility is the root that feeds the other virtues. You would have to buy and read a library full of contemporary Christian books to find statements like the following, beginning with Augustine (354–430):

> So if you ask me concerning the most important precepts of the Christian religion, first, second, third, and always I would answer "Humility." . . . Let no man flatter himself; *of himself he is Satan.* His blessing comes from God alone. For what do you have of your own but sin? . . . By God's mercy alone we stand, since by ourselves we are *nothing but evil.*[17]

A millennium later, the Reformer John Calvin (1509–64) wrote:

> I am compelled here to repeat once more: that whoever is utterly cast down and overwhelmed by the awareness of his calamity, poverty, nakedness, and disgrace has thus advanced farthest in knowledge of himself. . . . These [the Scriptures]

testify that no one is permitted to receive God's blessings unless he is consumed with the awareness of his own poverty.[18]

The great American theologian Jonathan Edwards (1703–58), one of my personal heroes, wrote:

The essence of evangelical humiliation consists in such humility as becomes a creature in itself exceedingly sinful, under a dispensation of grace; consisting in a mean esteem of himself, as in himself nothing, and altogether contemptible and odious; attended with a mortification of a disposition to exalt himself, and a free renunciation of his own glory. . . . This is a great and most essential thing in true religion. The whole frame of the gospel, everything appertaining to the new covenant, and all God's dispensations towards fallen man, are calculated to bring to pass this effect [humility]. They that are destitute of this have no true religion [Christianity] whatever profession they may make.[19]

Coming to the twentieth century, C. S. Lewis adds:

Whenever we find that our religious life is making us feel that we are good—above all, that we are better than someone else—I think we may be sure that we are being acted on not by God but by the Devil. The real test of being in the presence of God is that you either forget about yourself altogether or see yourself as a small, dirty object. It is better to forget about yourself altogether.[20]

When was the last time you heard people described as a "small, dirty object" or altogether "contemptible and odious"? When was the last time you heard a sermon on man's sinfulness or the wrath that man deserves? When was the last time you heard a sermon on hell? Many believers studiously avoid these subjects, and not always from malice, but through ignorance of man's problem and the appropriate solution. God's people desperately need to see themselves as did Job, Isaiah, and Peter. As we have seen, the conversion of unbelievers, the sanctification of God's people, and the favor of God depend on our capacity to advance in humility.

THE CROSS SPEAKS

Ultimately, the cross is the proof of this proposition. Jesus died in our place, as our substitute. On our behalf and in our place he died to satisfy God's justice. In other words, Christ got what we deserve. The Bible teaches that God humbles those who exalt themselves. Jesus received the humbling that our constant and unremitting self-exaltation merits. What does it deserve? Crucifixion! In other words, our self-exaltation is so heinous in God's sight that it must be crucified. That is the humbling our pride deserves! Jesus' abasement was astounding. Stripped naked, he was slowly and humiliatingly tortured to death. Onlookers jeered and mocked. All of this took place at Golgotha, which was probably the city garbage dump. Why? Because that is the humbling our pride deserves!

The cross speaks emphatically: "God hates pride! It is *extremely serious in God's sight.*" The cross strips us of all grounds for boasting. It says that our moral position is desperate. The cross convinces us to make Christ's substitutionary atonement our only boast. In other words, because of the cross, I can boast in God's love despite the complete absence of personal merit. I deserve damnation. My arrogance deserves to be humiliated in the shame of crucifixion. I should be at peace with myself and with God—not because I am humble, but despite the fact that I am proud. My self-image does not rest on my own performance. It rests on God's love for me *despite* my failure to perform. God designed salvation to deeply humble me, to crush my pride, and to transfer my grounds for positive self-image from self to God. If you ever doubt the seriousness of your hubris, look at the cross. It proclaims both the judgment I deserve and the love of God that is my boast and confidence.

MIGHTY STRUCTURES NEED DEEP FOUNDATIONS

A friend just won a contract to wire a ten-story office building. He went to the site and found a four-story chasm bored deep into the earth. Puzzled, he asked the architect about the hole and its depth. "The deeper the foundation, the higher the superstructure that we can build," the architect explained. This is what D. Martyn Lloyd-Jones had in mind when he wrote: "But the deeper you go in repentance, conviction, and agony of soul the more likely you are to be lifted to the heights."[21] The deeper we descend into the unpleasant truth about ourselves, the weightier the spiritual edifice that God can erect on our ministry or our church. Jesus summed it up with a simple expression repeated many times in the Bible: "Everyone who exalts himself will be humbled, and he who humbles himself will be exalted" (Luke 14:11). Do you want to experience increased intimacy with God? More fruitfulness? More conversions? More effective ministry? Clothe yourself in humility. Minister humility to others. Be an agent of humility to those you serve. "If you plan to build a tall house of virtues," wrote Augustine, "you must first lay deep foundations of humility."[22]

Everyone reading this chapter has the disease of pride. Are you willing to take God's diagnosis? Are you like Don, whose story opened this chapter: even though you feel healthy, might you have a terminal diagnosis? "Those who are well have no need of a physician," said Jesus, "but those who are sick" (Matt. 9:12).

Because we are all sick, even though we often feel healthy, God has designed the gospel to expose the nature and extent of our disease. How God structured the gospel to do that is the subject of the next section, chapters three through seven.

PART
TWO

THE GOSPEL THAT HUMBLES

We have renounced disgraceful, underhanded ways. We refuse to practice cunning or to tamper with God's word, but by the open statement of the truth we would commend ourselves to everyone's conscience in the sight of God.

—The Apostle Paul (2 Corinthians 4:1–2)

3

Humbled by the Wrath of God

Yet if we would know God, it is vital that we face the truth concerning his wrath, however unfashionable it may be, and however strong our initial prejudices against it. Otherwise we shall not understand the gospel of salvation from wrath, nor the propitiatory achievement of the cross, nor the wonder of the redeeming love of God.

—J. I. Packer[1]

CHAPTER 1 SUGGESTED that humility is the great virtue and pride the great evil. The other virtues—love, faithfulness, mercy, self-sacrifice, and so forth—all feed on humility. It is the fuel that sustains them. Humility is the ability to see ourselves and all of life as God does. Isaiah 66:1–2 tells us that God seeks humility, true contrition, and trembling at his Word. These three are progressive. Humility is crucial. It begins the process. It is necessary for both conversion and sanctification.

Chapter 2 examined our contemporary infatuation with self. We examined contemporary culture through the lens of social psychology, the clear teaching of the Bible, and the testimony of past Christian greats. We are in trouble, and the gospel that humbles is the answer.

Because we are naturally arrogant, God designed the gospel to humble us. The gospel begins with a humbling message. We are under the wrath of God.

I was visiting with a Christian friend. For some reason, our conversation turned to the wrath of God. Another friend—one whom I deeply love—was standing a few feet away. He is very religious. He is a longtime church attender. I could tell that he was listening in on our conversation. A few minutes later the interloper walked away, snorting, "I can't believe any rational person, living in the modern world, could actually believe that God and wrath go together." He was upset. Since that time, tension has marked our relationship.

Although his reaction hurt deeply, it did not surprise me. There is nothing more countercultural, more humbling (and sometimes more confusing) than the wrath of God. We are all, especially the non-Christian, convinced that God is love. But *wrath*? The word is like a spiritual stun gun, like an ice-water shower on a hot summer day.

Nevertheless, God's wrath is the subject of this chapter. We must deal with it. "One of the most striking things about the Bible," notes Dr. J. I. Packer, "is the vigor with which both Testaments emphasize the reality and terror of God's wrath. A study of the concordance will show that there are *more* references in Scripture to the anger, fury, and wrath of God, than there are to His love and tenderness."[2]

We must deal with the subject for a second reason. As upside down as this may sound, the wrath of God is essential to our happiness. It is difficult to find real enduring rest in your relationship with God, or security in his love, until you fully embrace the biblical teaching about God's wrath. In addition, we can trace most apathy about Christ and Christianity back to a failure to teach on the wrath of God. The doctrine of God's wrath makes us needy, and needy people are red-hot for Christ and his kingdom.

God's wrath is an important part of Paul's gospel. In this chapter and the next three, we are going to explore how Paul preached the gospel—and wrath is where he started.

We know this from the first three chapters of his letter to the Romans. There, Paul describes how he communicated his gospel. He begins in Romans 1:16–17 (quoting Hab. 2:4) with a clear statement of the gospel:

> For I am not ashamed of the gospel, for it is the power of God for salvation to everyone who believes, to the Jew first and also to the Greek. For in it the righteousness of God is revealed from faith for faith, as it is written, "The righteous shall live by faith."

Yet Paul knows that, by itself, this statement is not enough. His reader is proud, and his pride has blindfolded him. The first thing to which he is blind is his spiritual peril. He is ignorant of God, his own sinfulness, and his eternal problem, a problem compared to which all others are trivial—a broken relationship with God. Paul also knows that pride will make him reluctant to admit his problem.

Therefore, Paul announces the good news and takes a detour. From Romans 1:18 to Romans 3:20, he labors to impress his reader with what I call the bad news. The bad news begins with the wrath of God (1:18–32). Paul moves on to prove that we are all guilty of the sins for which we criticize others (2:1–11). He describes the accounting we will give to the law of God on the day of judgment (2:12–29). After showing that the benefits of being a Jew do not necessarily include salvation (3:1–8), he pivots to prove that all mankind is under the weight of sin (3:9–20). His conclusion? On the day of judgment, all mouths will be stopped. No one will be able to give God an excuse. All will stand condemned. All will agree that God's judgments are just (3:19–20).

Only then does Paul return to the gospel, in Romans 3:21–26.

In other words, Paul begins his presentation of the gospel with bad news. In fact, the bad news dominates his explanation of the gospel. From Romans 1:18 to 3:20 in the ESV version of the English Bible, there are 1,262 words to convince the Romans of their problem. Only then does he conclude with a presentation of the good news in six short verses (3:21–26). If we add up the two statements about the good news that bracket the bad news, 1:16–17 and 3:21–26, we have only 188 words devoted to the good news, but between these two statements we have the 1,262 words devoted to the bad news. There are almost seven words of bad news for every word about the good news.

This should not surprise us. Paul is attempting to batter down the doors of pride so that the clean breezes of illumination can enter. In chapter 1 we saw that humility is the ability to see things as God sees them. Therefore, our ability to see and hear the gospel will be according to our humbling. Humility removes the blindfold. That is why Paul devotes so much energy to the bad news. He wants us to see ourselves and God as we really are.

If we carefully read Paul's letters in their chronological order, we find confirmation that this was in fact how Paul consistently presented his gospel.

PRELUDE TO ROMANS

In AD 51, Paul wrote his first preserved letter. His urgency about the wrath of God was already apparent. He exhorted the Thessalonians "to wait for his Son from heaven, whom he raised from the dead, Jesus who delivers us from the wrath to come" (1 Thess. 1:10). Then he closed this letter, "God has not destined us for wrath, but to obtain salvation through our Lord Jesus Christ" (1 Thess. 5:9). From the beginning of his ministry Paul was clear about one thing: the gospel solves our greatest human need, freedom from the wrath of God.

A couple of years later, in about AD 54 or 55, Paul wrote his letter to the Galatians. First, he reminded them that there was something inherently offensive about his gospel, especially his understanding of the cross, something that made it responsible for most of his persecution. "But if I, brothers, still preach circumcision, why am I still being persecuted? In that case the *offense of the cross* has been removed" (Gal. 5:11). Preaching circumcision was code for "you are good enough to earn it," and it provoked little offense. But preaching the cross assumed human bankruptcy and the wrath that was God's response. It was inherently offensive.

More insight comes from Galatians 6:12: "It is those who want to make a good showing in the flesh who would force you to be circumcised, and only in order that they may *not be persecuted* for the cross of Christ." Paul was under no illusions. Preaching the gospel, "the cross of Christ" (refusing to preach circumcision), was the accelerant that ignited most of his persecutions. The way to get around this persecution was to preach circumcision—that is, God is not really upset. You are not that bad. You can earn his favor by trying a little harder.

Two years passed. Sometime between AD 55 and 57, Paul wrote to the church at Corinth. Here we gain even more insights.

> And I, when I came to you, brothers, did not come proclaiming to you the testimony of God with lofty speech or wisdom.

61

> For I decided to know nothing among you except Jesus Christ
> and him crucified. And I was with you *in weakness and in fear
> and much trembling.* (1 Cor. 2:1–3)

We learn two things from these words. Paul's message was
Christ crucified, and he entered Corinth "in weakness and
in fear and much trembling." What was it about "Jesus Christ
and him crucified" that caused such anxiety? It was not the
message that Jesus loves you and has a wonderful plan for
your life. It was the humbling nature of his gospel, a humbling
that provoked persecution, and a humbling that Paul's gospel
intended to produce.

Within a year or two, Paul wrote a second letter to the
church at Corinth. In it he reminded the Corinthians that
his gospel was "the aroma of Christ to God among those who
are being saved and among those who are perishing, to one a
fragrance from death to death, to the other a fragrance from
life to life. Who is sufficient for these things?" (2 Cor. 2:15–16).
To those being saved, the gospel smelled like an irresistibly
attractive perfume. To others, it was just a message about a
dead man. It smelled like a rotting corpse. There was no middle
ground, and there were no bored listeners. What caused both
the positive and the negative reactions? It was the bad news
that always preceded Paul's preaching of the good news. He
progressed to the judgment to come. Here is how he noted its
effect on himself: "For we must all appear before the judgment
seat of Christ, so that each one may receive what is due for
what he has done in the body, whether good or evil. Therefore,
knowing the fear of the Lord, we persuade others" (5:10–11).

Then we have Paul's stupendous persecutions chronicled
at the end of 2 Corinthians:

> Three times I was beaten with rods. Once I was stoned. Three
> times I was shipwrecked; a night and a day I was adrift at sea; on
> frequent journeys, in danger from rivers, danger from robbers,

danger from my own people, danger from Gentiles, danger in the city, danger in the wilderness, danger at sea, danger from false brothers; in toil and hardship, through many a sleepless night, in hunger and thirst, often without food, in cold and exposure. And, apart from other things, there is the daily pressure on me of my anxiety for all the churches. (2 Cor. 11:25–28)

And these sufferings were just the beginning. They were recorded before many of his later sufferings in Acts occurred. Paul would later experience a beating by a mob in Jerusalem, imprisonment in Caesarea for two years, shipwreck on Malta, imprisonment in Rome for two years, and the confinement during which he wrote his second letter to Timothy. This provokes an important question: What inspired this terrific opposition? It was not the promise of "your best life now." It was the call to humility latent in Paul's gospel. It was a gospel that started with the wrath of God, the looming reality of judgment, the utter sinfulness of man, the penal substitutionary atonement, and the utter bankruptcy of all attempts to earn God's favor by performance. Its benefits were available only to those who renounced all confidence in their good works and cast themselves by faith upon Christ's cross and resurrection.

By the time we reach AD 57–58, and the letter to the Romans, we expect an explanation. What caused Paul's persecutions? What provoked the divisions, the offenses, and the scandals? For the first time, in systematic written form, Paul describes how he communicated his gospel. In other words, he explains the architecture of his gospel—how he preached it. We see why it offended, why it provoked such persecution, and why it divided. The source of these problems was the bad news explained in Romans 1:18–3:20. And the bad news begins with wrath. Ironically, it was this very offense that brought God's power so radically to bear on those who heard. Paul preached the gospel this way, "that your faith might not rest in the wisdom of men but in the power of God" (1 Cor. 2:5).

HUMBLING BEGINS WITH WRATH

Paul knew that the good news is a big yawn to those who do not understand their plight, and no one understands this naturally. We are like a car moving at 70 mph toward an invisible concrete wall. We are unaware of our peril. Pride has blinded us. We cannot see the wall, but that doesn't change the fact that it is there. Gospel preaching makes the wall visible.

Paul begins his discussion of wrath in Romans 1:18: "For the wrath of God is revealed from heaven against all ungodliness and unrighteousness of men, who by their unrighteousness suppress the truth." Paul is not embarrassed about God's wrath. He does not apologize for it. He does not even explain it. He just lays it out. That is because God himself is not embarrassed about his wrath. It is one important expression of his moral perfections.

As I experienced with my friend, all you have to do is to mention the wrath of God and hackles will rise. Why do people get so upset about the wrath of God? There are several reasons.

First, human wrath is sinful. It is often self-centered and out of control. Wrath implies intense, unrestrained, spontaneous anger, the kind that causes damage. If God is sinless, how can his wrath be virtuous?

But the premise that wrath is always sinful is faulty. For example, Paul tells us to "be angry and do not sin" (Eph. 4:26). Anger is not inherently wrong. Anger can be either sinful or virtuous. Only sinful anger is wrong, and God's wrath is never sinful. In fact, it is an essential aspect of his goodness. We can have no confidence that God is infinitely good, I mean good in a way that we can utterly bank our entire lives upon, unless he gets angry, really angry, at sin and evil.

In addition, there is a difference between God's anger and ours. The Bible goes to great lengths to remind us that God is "slow to anger" (Ex. 34:6). His wrath is never unrestrained or capricious. It does not erupt suddenly. Rather, it is his settled determination to show intense hostility toward evil in every form. In addition, the objects of his anger always deserve it.

We would all agree that a perfectly good Being must love virtue with an infinite passion. Likewise, if sin destroys lives, eviscerates human happiness, and robs God of his glory, then an infinitely good Being must hate evil in all its forms. If evil is this destructive, how could God be passive toward it and be good?

For example, a "good" God could not be passive about the Holocaust. In the presence of evil, anyone really good must take sides, or he is not good. In the same way, we would not call someone "good" who was indifferent to the sexual abuse of a child or the rape of its mother. It would be difficult to convince you that someone passive toward the rape of a child was good. You might call him a marshmallow, but you wouldn't call him good. We want just the opposite. We expect goodness to be angry, to get worked up, to take sides, to punish the offender. We want Adolf Hitler punished. We want Joseph Stalin punished. We want Idi Amin punished. We want this because we are made in God's image, and God wants them punished.

God is not a marshmallow. He is infinitely good. Therefore, he opposes evil. He gets angry. In fact, the Greek word for this anger is so fraught with emotion that we must translate it "wrath." It is a strong word. After thinking all this through, anyone who is honest will admit that we don't really object to God's getting angry. We object to his getting angry *with us*. We are proud. Our real objection is not that God gets angry. Our problem is that *we don't think we are evil.* We think Hitler was evil and deserves God's wrath, but our sins seem minuscule and insignificant by comparison. Hitler was bad, but deep down inside we are convinced that we are good.

Yet the Bible is clear. God is angry with everyone outside of Christ, and his wrath is not a minor subject. "In the Old Testament," notes Leon Morris, "more than twenty words are used of the wrath of God. . . . The total number of references to God's wrath exceeds 580, so that it cannot be said to be an occasional topic. . . . In the Bible the wrath of God is intensely personal."[3]

There is a second reason that the wrath of God upsets us. We don't know how to harmonize God's love and wrath. John 3:16 tells us that "God so loved the world, that he gave his only Son," but Romans 1:18 tells us that "the wrath of God is revealed." In our thinking these are polar opposites, and yet Scripture is clear. God simultaneously feels both intense love and intense wrath for fallen sinners. He loves those with whom he is angry, and that is what makes his love so wonderful. It is love for enemies. "The Bible can simultaneously affirm God's wrath toward people and his love for them," observes D. A. Carson. "It does not intimate that God's love and his judicial 'hatred' are necessarily mutually exclusive. So why should love and hatred be exclusive in us?"[4]

God's love saves us from God's wrath. "Since, therefore, we have now been justified by his blood, much more shall we be saved by him from the wrath of God" (Rom. 5:9). God saves sinners from his own wrath. He saves them from himself. He does this because he loves them. God feels the most intense love for those for whom he also feels the most intense wrath. We will come back to this idea before we close this chapter. Ultimately, both the love of God and the wrath of God are reconciled and mutually glorified in the cross of Christ.

THE WRATH OF GOD IS PERSONAL

C. H. Dodd (1884–1973) popularized the idea that God's wrath is impersonal. It is just the working out of the laws of cause and effect, the sowing and reaping that people experience as a consequence of normal living in a fallen world. If a man commits adultery, he will reap anger from his wife. But Dodd suggests that God is not personally angry toward him.[5]

The picture presented in Scripture, however, is exactly the opposite. The wrath of God is intensely personal. We are not pantheists. We worship a personal God. He has feelings. He gets angry. Unbelievers can experience this wrath in several ways.

Unbelievers experience God's wrath when he gives them up to their lusts. Someone wants something badly enough, and persists in wanting it for long enough, and God eventually gives him up to it, and sometimes with no hope of deliverance. This is how Paul describes first-century culture in Romans chapter 1. The Gentiles worshiped humanity—man made himself the measure of all things. How did God respond? He gave them up to homosexuality and sexual impurity (Rom. 1:18–32). The growing homosexual movement is proof that our culture is under God's wrath.

The wrath of God comes to unbelievers in another way—spiritual blindness and deafness. God shuts down the eyes and ears of their hearts, making it impossible for them to hear from him. They are now blind and deaf, unable to respond to God's Word. This is one way Israel experienced the wrath of God in the eighth century BC. After Isaiah saw "the Lord . . . high and lifted up" (Isa. 6:1), God gave him this unpleasant commission:

Go, and say to this people:

"Keep on hearing, but do not understand;
keep on seeing, but do not perceive."

Make the heart of this people dull,
    and their ears heavy,
    and blind their eyes;
lest they see with their eyes,
    and hear with their ears,
and understand with their hearts,
    and turn and be healed. (Isa. 6:9–10)

Israel's punishment for its persistent idolatry was the blindness and deafness that follow a hardened heart.[6] More than anything else, we should fear this manifestation of God's anger. Israel was still under this judgment in Jesus' day. In fact, when asked why he spoke to them in parables, Jesus quoted this passage from Isaiah. In essence, he said, "I speak in parables to obfuscate the truth. I speak in parables to fulfill God's judgment pronounced through Isaiah long ago. I speak in parables so that Israel cannot understand." (See Matt. 13:10–17.)

A third way that our fallen world experiences God's wrath is through national calamity. God expressed his wrath through the Babylonian conquest of Jerusalem in 587 B.C. "But because our fathers had angered the God of heaven, he gave them into the hand of Nebuchadnezzar king of Babylon, the Chaldean, who destroyed this house and carried away the people to Babylonia" (Ezra 5:12).

A fourth way in which unbelievers can experience the wrath of God is through sowing and reaping. When sexual promiscuity terminates in genital herpes, the wrath of God is at work. "Let no one deceive you with empty words, for because of these things [e.g., sexual immorality] the wrath of God comes upon the sons of disobedience" (Eph. 5:6).

Fifth, wrath can be experienced through sickness, disease, or death. I am not saying that these are always direct indications of God's personal wrath. They are not. In general they are a judgment for Adam's sin, a judgment dispensed to the human race at large. All of God's favorites, his saints, will eventually get sick and die. I am referring to specific instances when God judges people with premature death or sickness. For example, God's anger burned against King Ahab and his wife Jezebel. It terminated in both of their deaths and the deaths of all seventy of their descendants (2 Kings 9:30–10:17).

Most distressing, all unbelievers experience the wrath of God as eternal damnation—eternal conscious suffering in hell with no hope. Hell exists to glorify God's wrath and justice, to convince us of its reasonableness, to magnify the serious-ness of our sin, and to convince us of the intensely personal nature of God's anger toward both us and our sin (Isa. 66:24; Mark 9:45–49).

In summary, wrath matters. The gospel is the solution to our most basic problem—the bad news. The wrath of God is its first dimension. This is why Paul described the gospel in two verses (Rom. 1:16–17) and quickly shifted to a long dissertation on the wrath of God. Only needy people believe and repent. Without the knowledge of God's wrath, Paul's readers would feel little need for the gospel. As Martin Luther observed:

> The gospel tastes best to those who lie in the straits of death, or whom an evil conscience oppresses. For in that case hunger is a good cook as we say, one who makes the food taste good. For when they feel their misery, the heart and conscience can hear nothing more soothing than the gospel; for this they long, on this they are eager to feed, nor can they get too much of it. . . . But that hardened class who live in their own holiness, build on their own works, and feel not their sin and misery do not taste this food. Whoever sits at a table and is hungry relishes all; however, he who is sated relishes nothing but is filled with loathing at the most excellent food.[7]

Wrath also matters because, as we will see in a later chap-ter, we must go through the wrath of God to get to the love of God. We must walk through this door to grasp the divine love in which Paul exults. God hides his love in his wrath. Until we face the wrath of God with all its disturbing implications, we cannot see, understand, or really appreciate the love of God. Without it, God's love will be just a superhuman form of affection. It will not be the "love . . . that surpasses knowledge" that Paul described in Ephesians 3:19. "The truth is," writes David Powlison, "you can't understand God's love if you don't understand His anger."[8]

OBJECTIONS TO THE WRATH OF GOD

In the 1960s the great missionary Roland Allen wrote, "We have lost the sense that the Judge is at the door and that the wrath of God against all ungodliness is ready to be revealed. We no longer look upon the acceptance of our message as 'deliverance from the wrath to come.' "[9] A quick survey of the evangelical church at the beginning of the twenty-first century suggests that Allen spoke prophetically. Most evangelicals have never heard a sermon on the wrath of God, have not heard a presentation of the gospel in the context of God's wrath, or can even find the wrath of God on their short list of significant theological topics. For most of us, it is an embarrassment. This is a problem. You can't read the Bible seriously without continual confrontation with the wrath of God. Despite this, it has become the W-word, one not mentioned in polite company. Let me suggest several reasons why this is the case, and why we need to reverse this trend.

On the street, I ran into two Christian brothers whom I have known for years. They go to a popular seeker-sensitive church in our area. They believe Jesus died for their sins, and for that I am thankful. But that is about as deep as it goes. They have never heard a sermon on God's wrath. They know little of the bad news. Their spirituality is predictable. Their pride has not been touched. Therefore, they feel little need for God. They have little zeal for Christ and his kingdom. At best they are spiritual infants. If I asked their pastor why he did not address the wrath of God regularly, he would probably give me one of the following reasons—many of them sincerely held. His ignorance is probably sincere ignorance, but nevertheless, it is an ignorance that hurts the cause of Christ.

First, he might believe that new converts are not ready for the wrath of God. On one level he is probably right. But is anyone ever ready for this subject? If you are waiting for a time when believers will be ready, you will be disappointed. They will never be ready. This subject always humbles, and no amount of sitting in a church pew is going to make it less humbling or acceptable. More importantly, this was not the approach of Paul or the other apostles. As we saw in Romans, Paul's standard gospel to unbelievers, and spiritual infants, *began* with the wrath of God. We already noted how Paul's first letter to the Thessalonians, a church only a couple of months old, assumed their knowledge of God's wrath. Although they were all new converts, he referenced the wrath of God three times (1 Thess. 1:10; 2:16; 5:9), and he did so as if his readers already understood that escaping God's wrath was a basic rationale for their faith. This is where Paul's gospel began.

Second, the seeker-sensitive pastor might avoid preaching about the wrath of God because it offends. The wrath of God means that my opinion of myself is too high. It means that I am not the good person I always thought I was. It means that God does not grade on a curve. It means that I will not get into heaven by being as good as, or a little better than, those around me. It means that no matter how good I feel about myself, I am in profound trouble. In addition, if I accept the wrath of God, I will be different. It will set me apart from my unbelieving friends, who are still under the wrath of God. Their pride of life will persecute me.

It does not help to wait until people have made a profession of faith. Believers are no different. The wrath of God deeply offends them also. But if they are true believers, if they are called by God, they will humble themselves under this subject. All true conversions involve "stooping." True believers hear, believe, and stoop. They bow low in worship.

Ultimately, the willingness to discuss God's wrath is a matter of faith. In what or whom do I trust? Do I rely on my cleverness and persuasiveness to convert others, or do I rely on the power of God? Those who trust in the power of God begin with the wrath of God. They want to produce a humbling faith, so they let the bad news do its work. They do not dwell on the wrath of God more than necessary. The wrath of God is never an end in itself. They start here in order to unwrap the grace and love of God that "[surpass] knowledge" (Eph. 3:19). In the words of John Bradford (1510–55), "If you will go to heaven you must sail by hell."[10]

Third, the pastor might avoid the wrath of God because it divides. He is right. It divides religious people (those who refuse to humble themselves, today's Pharisees) from those truly born again. Jesus' sheep hear his voice. Jesus' sheep humble themselves under this message, but religious people get angry.

Fourth, he might not discuss the wrath of God because he assumes that fire and brimstone (i.e., fear of punishment) has no place in the conversion of people. He is partly right. Fundamentally, conversion is a response to the love, mercy, and grace of God. My contention, however, is that you cannot get to the love, mercy, and grace of God until you thoroughly explain what people deserve. To do that, you must start with the wrath of God. Once again, the wrath of God is not an end in itself. It is a bridge to the extravagant love, mercy, and grace of God.

Fifth, such a pastor might reason, "If I start with the wrath of God, my congregation will get smaller, and no one will ever be converted. My ministry will be over." It might get smaller. Your ministry might be over. But preserving your life or ministry is never supposed to be your goal. Losing our lives for the gospel's sake is our goal. Only he who loses his life will save it (Matt. 16:25).

The person who makes this objection might really be saying, "I trust in my cleverness and arguments to win people to Christ. I want a gospel that does not offend or divide." But there is nothing clever or sophisticated about the gospel. It is a "stumbling block" (1 Cor. 1:23), a cause of persecution (Gal. 6:12), utter foolishness to worldly sophistication (1 Cor. 1:20–21). It is scandalous (1 Cor. 1:23) to all that is popular. If this is your objection, might you love the "work of the Lord" more than the "Lord of the work"? Is it possible that a growing congregation has become an idol, that the love of worldly "success" has seduced you?

Sixth, he might not discuss the wrath of God because he doesn't want the label *fundamentalist*. This is a reasonable fear. Some will call you a fundamentalist. In fact, they will probably call you worse. Yet this is an opportunity to share in the Master's sufferings. He was hated by the Jews (John 7:7). His own family thought he was "out of his mind" (Mark 3:20–21). The Pharisees persecuted him. Those he grew up with rejected him (Luke 4:16–29). Everyone routinely misunderstood him, even his own disciples. And eventually, his peers crucified him! "All who desire to live a godly life in Christ Jesus will be persecuted" (2 Tim. 3:12).

Finally, the pastor might not discuss the wrath of God because he is afraid his congregation won't bring their friends. Sometimes members of my congregation, even those who love our church, say something like this: "I will bring my friends here after they have been Christians for a while, but I don't think they can handle the message. It is too counter-cultural." If their real objection is that my communication skills are poor, I thank them for their criticism. But if their real objection is "I am embarrassed by the gospel," or "I don't trust God to work through the bad news," then I usually respond with something like this: "Is it possible that you are ashamed of the gospel?" Or I might respond, "Are you saying that smooth arguments and sophisticated reasoning converts people?" Sometimes I ask, "Do you believe that true conversions occur by the power of God's Spirit, and that God is most apt to release that power when we are sincerely and plainly honest with people about their predicament? Or do you believe that conversions are the result of apologetics and smooth arguments?"

Remember, two verses before Romans 1:18, Paul said, "I am not ashamed of the gospel, for it is the power of God for salvation" (Rom. 1:16). Paul was probably tempted to be ashamed. Why? His gospel began with God's wrath. This subject has never been popular. "According to the Bible," notes Mark Dever, "evangelism may not be defined in terms of results or methods, but only in terms of *faithfulness to the message preached*. . . . We don't fail in our evangelism if we faithfully present the Gospel and yet the person is not converted; we fail only if we don't faithfully present the Gospel at all."[11] In his wonderful book *The Old Evangelicalism*, Iain Murray writes, "Wheresoever God works with power for salvation upon the minds of men, there will be some discoveries of a sense of sin, of the danger of the wrath of God. . . . The knowledge of God does not first come to sinners with comfort, rather it is intensely disturbing."[12]

If we are honest with ourselves, we will confess that one of the reasons for our weakness, tepidness, and failure to speak the truth is embarrassment. We are ashamed of the gospel. Ultimately, that is why we ignore or change the bad news.

THE WRATH OF GOD IS THE FIRST STEP IN OUR HUMBLING

Let's return to the thesis of this book. Saving faith always involves some humbling. Again, I am not saying that we are saved by humility. We are saved by faith alone. What I am saying is that what we believe, the content of our faith, should serve to humble us. The more we are humbled, the better. The wrath of God, a clear understanding of what I deserve, is the first ingredient in a humbling faith.

Chapter 1 noted that humility is the root from which all the other virtues grow. Because the wrath of God humbles us, it amplifies our capacity to love God and man. It equips us to understand the "breadth and length and height and depth" of God's love "that surpasses knowledge" (Eph. 3:18–19). Those who feel this love begin to exercise it. They grow in kindness, charity, gentleness, and grace. Gratitude is their calling card. They know that they deserve crucifixion, and they are thankful that they are not getting it. Those who accept the wrath of God forgive 70 times 7 and 24/7. If Jesus forgave me when I was an object of his wrath, how can I cling to bitterness? Those who accept the wrath of God love their enemies. If God the Father sent his Son to die for his enemies, for those under his wrath, the recipients of this love are compelled to do the same.

Those who emphasize God's wrath love God more. Preaching the wrath of God cures lukewarmness. "I was God's enemy, subject to his wrath. In that state Christ died for me." Those who are loved this way feel a great debt to God. They love him in return.

This was Jesus' point in the story about the sinful woman. Weeping, she anointed Jesus with perfume. She knew the great sins for which she had been forgiven, and how unworthy she was. That is why she extravagantly "wasted" her perfume on

75

Jesus. "She loved much," Jesus said, "but he who is forgiven little, loves little" (Luke 7:47). In the same way, those who accept God's wrath know that they have been forgiven much, and they love much. The sure way to lull people into lukewarmness is to conceal this truth from them.

WRATH AND THE CROSS

Maybe you are a Christian, but you are a skeptic about the content of this chapter. To you it all seems a bit exaggerated. May I take you to the cross of Christ? The cross puts a profound exclamation mark on all that I have said about the wrath of God.

Remember, the cross works by penal substitution.[13] Those two words *penal* and *substitution* are very important.

Substitution refers to our union with Christ. Jesus came to earth as a substitute for all who believe the gospel. He lived a perfect life for us. When we believe, God unites us with him and imputes his perfections to us.

Penal refers to the idea that, because of this union, Jesus was able to take the penalty that we deserve. Not only is Christ's righteousness imputed to us, but our sins are imputed to Christ. As we have seen, the penalty that our sin deserves is the wrath of God. So Jesus suffered the wrath of God in our place. That is what the cross was—a demonstration of what God's wrath looks like. It is a picture of God's holiness, his hatred of sin, and his anger toward both sin and sinners. On the cross, God's Son bore the demands of God's justice in our place.

Some think the wrath of God is nothing but impersonal sowing and reaping. But on the cross, Jesus got the wrath we deserve. The penalty, the judgment, the suffering from God was personal. God sent it to punish guilty individuals. The words of the prophet Isaiah describe this "penalty":

Surely he has borne our griefs
    and carried our sorrows;
yet we esteemed him stricken,
    smitten by God, and afflicted.
But he was wounded for our transgressions;
    he was crushed for our iniquities;
upon him was the chastisement that brought us peace,
    and with his stripes we are healed.
All we like sheep have gone astray;
    we have turned—every one—to his own way;
and the LORD has laid on him
    the iniquity of us all.

He was oppressed, and he was afflicted,
    yet he opened not his mouth;
like a lamb that is led to the slaughter,
    and like a sheep that before its shearers is silent,
    so he opened not his mouth. (Isa. 53:4–7)

Notice the words of substitution: "Wounded for our transgressions; . . . crushed for our iniquities; . . . The LORD has laid on him the iniquity of us all." Verse 10 takes us to the heart of the matter: "It was the will of the LORD to crush him."

Jesus' sufferings were not just a matter of sowing and reaping. It was all very personal. God was angry. We deserved to be crushed. But God the Father so loved the world that he crushed his Son in our place. The prophet Zechariah adds more insight: " 'Awake, O sword, against my shepherd, against the man who stands next to me,' declares the LORD of hosts. 'Strike the shepherd, and the sheep will be scattered' " (Zech. 13:7). God the Father withdrew the sword from his scabbard and struck down his Son so that he wouldn't have to strike us. It was active and personal. Because the Son bore our sin, God the Father "crushed" him. As the crushing was ending, the Father administered the final blow. He abandoned his Son. He abandoned him because that is what our sins deserve—utter abandonment in hell forever. "My God, my God, why have you forsaken me?" Jesus cried as he sank into the unconsciousness of physical death (Matt. 27:46).

The cross shows us what God's wrath looks like, and it is not pleasant. There is no way to adequately describe it with human words, and there is no way to clean it up or remove its offense. It was infinite suffering, the suffering that only an infinite Being has the capacity to absorb. In a previous book I wrote:

> There is almost no way to exaggerate crucifixion's brutality. Even the cruel, ruthless Roman government crucified only the lowest social classes—slaves and commoners. A Roman citizen could be beheaded for capital crime but never crucified. It was too demeaning. Because Paul was a Roman citizen he was probably beheaded, but Peter, a commoner, was crucified (upside down, according to legend). The cross was so distasteful that Cicero said it should never be mentioned in polite company. To the Jews it was a sign of God's cursing. It was a breathtakingly humiliating death, which usually took place near garbage dumps or similarly degraded locations.
>
> The victim was nailed or tied to a cross that was then impaled into the ground. The condemned was left to die a slow death from thirst and exposure. It was lingering, agonizing, torture, and because the loss of blood was minimal, death usually took several days. The fastest recorded deaths were after thirty-six hours. In some cases, the executioners broke the victims' legs, crushed their ribs, or scourged them to hasten death. They showed Jesus this mercy.
>
> Convulsions usually set in, and each movement tore the victim's hands and feet against the raw wounds.[14] The pain was excruciating. Because the offender cried out for death, soldiers were stationed around the cross to prevent friends from killing the convicted or freeing him by force.

To enhance the humiliation, the malefactor often was crucified naked. The authorities usually nailed a placard over
the cross, broadcasting the crime for which the criminal suffered. It might read "stealing," "murder," or "insurrection."
In Jesus' case it read, "King of the Jews." He was crucified for
telling the truth.[15]

The cross points us to a hell of eternal, personal, conscious
torment. The cross speaks clearly. It proclaims the horrors
of God's wrath up front and personal. Blood, sweat, agony,
shame, and mind-numbing pain are its physical dimensions.

WRATH OUR FRIEND

But the cross is also the measure of God's love, and it is an
astounding love. We see it through the lens of God's wrath.
That is because God's love is love for enemies. The truth about
God's wrath makes that point clear. God loves those for whom
he feels enmity. He acts to remove the enmity, to reconcile us
and make us his friends.

It is natural for us to love our friends. Even members of
the Mafia make sacrifices for family members and friends. We
don't sacrifice and suffer for our enemies. We reject them.
Here is where God differs. He died for his enemies, and the
price paid was infinite. He gave his Son to save people "by
nature children of wrath" (Eph. 2:3). In the words of D. A.
Carson, "Do you want to see the greatest evidence of the love of
God? Go to the cross. Do you want to see the greatest evidence
of the justice of God? Go to the cross. It is where wrath and
mercy meet. Holiness and peace kiss each other. The climax
of redemptive history is the cross."[16]

The wrath of God is also the key to assurance. The connection is powerful. If God loved you because you were good,
that is, the wrath of God was a fiction, then his love would

be conditional. He would love you because you perform. It follows that the failure to perform would also result in the withdrawal of his love.

But if God loved you by sending his Son to be tortured to death in your place, and if he did this for creatures deserving of his wrath, and if he did this to remove the wrath and make you his friend, then you will never feel insecure about his love. Why? God's love is not conditional. It is not based on your performance. Just the opposite. He loved you despite the complete absence of performance. He died for you when he was angry with you. He did this because he wanted to be your friend, because he wanted to propitiate his anger. If this is true, how can your failures, sins, and inconsistencies ever separate you from his love and affection? The answer is obvious. This is Paul's point in Romans 5:10: "For if while we were enemies we were reconciled to God by the death of his Son, much more, now that we are reconciled, shall we be saved by his life."

That is why those who fail to communicate the wrath of God produce lukewarm Christians. The truth about God's wrath exposes our need. The Laodicean church in Revelation 3 is famous for its spiritual tepidness. "I know your works," said Jesus. "You are neither cold nor hot. Would that you were either cold or hot! So, because you are lukewarm, and neither hot nor cold, I will spit you out of my mouth" (Rev. 3:15–16). Why were the Laodiceans lukewarm? They did not understand their need. "For you say, I am rich, I have prospered, and I need nothing, not realizing that you are wretched, pitiable, poor, blind, and naked" (3:17). These words describe many Christians today. The bad news is the cure, and the wrath of God is at the heart of the bad news. It exposes our need. It motivates zeal for Christ and his kingdom.

So in the end, the wrath of God becomes our friend. It defines and expands God's love. It is the ground of our assurance, and it motivates zeal for Christ and his kingdom.

SUMMARY

The wrath of God is a humbling subject, but it is necessary. It is a difficult subject. It should be explained with great tenderness and compassion. If you discuss the wrath of God with Christians, share the wrath of God with unbelievers, counsel the wrath of God to the hurting, or preach the wrath of God, you will sometimes get the response that I got from my relative—anger and hostility. At other times, however, you will gain converts—true, solid, substantial, enduring converts—whose rock-solid faith is built on a foundation of growing humility. "But the LORD is the true God; he is the living God and the everlasting King. At his wrath the earth quakes, and the nations cannot endure his indignation" (Jer. 10:10).

Paul understood this principle. As we have seen, the first three chapters of Romans devote seven words to the bad news for every word about the good news. Paul did this because he understood our resistance to the bad news. The heart is desperately wicked and deceitful.

Don't be deceived. God's wrath is personal. Many objections have been advanced against this teaching. This chapter has attempted to disarm them.

Ultimately, the wrath of God culminates in the New Testament. It culminates at the cross of Christ. The measure of God's wrath is the cross. The justification of God's wrath is the cross. What makes the love of God so indescribably wonderful is that it is love measured out to enemies, men and women by nature God's enemies (Rom. 5:10).

The wrath of God, however, is only the beginning of the bad news. Romans 2 informs the reader of the looming reality of the final judgment. We must all stand before the judgment seat of Christ. This sobering truth is the subject of chapter 4.

4

Humbled by Final Judgment

The great seriousness of the reality of being human, the dreadful seriousness of the coming judgment of God, the sheer insignificance of the present in the light of eternity—realities that once were the subtext of virtually every sermon—have now disappeared, and have been replaced by one triviality after another.

—T. David Gordon[1]

IF YOU HAD A CHANCE TO present the gospel to a roomful of philosophy majors at Harvard University, would you emphasize the final judgment? If you had a chance to publicly share the gospel with the governor of your state and his assembled staff, would you warn them of the judgment to come? Not many of us would even think to begin there. It would take great courage. But that is exactly what Paul did.

The Areopagus was the council that ruled Athens. Its prestige was great, going back centuries. It was the forum for the social elites, the roundtable for the secular intelligentsia of the first-century Roman world.

When asked to share the Christian message with the Areopagus, Paul spoke with amazing boldness. He didn't speak of God's love. He didn't make lavish promises of a happy, trouble-free life. Instead, he warned the listeners of the judgment to come. At the climax of his testimony, he told them that God "has fixed a day on which he will judge the world in righteousness by a man whom he has appointed; and of this he has given assurance to all by raising him from the dead" (Acts 17:31). People were not different then. Times have not changed. First-century intellectuals were not more open to news about a final judgment. The members of the Areopagus were just as offended as a group of Harvard philosophers would be today.

A few years later, Paul had the opportunity to share the gospel with Felix, the governor of Judea. Felix was the man who replaced Pontius Pilate. Like most other Roman governors, he was ruthless, self-centered, and self-serving. Paul was under Felix's control. He was in Felix's prison. Humanly speaking, it was in his best interest to ingratiate himself with Felix. Instead, when given an opportunity to defend himself to Felix, Paul "reasoned about righteousness and self-control and the coming judgment" (Acts 24:25).

Why did Paul discuss the final judgment? Because his presentation of the gospel flowed out of very specific assumptions about God and man. The final judgment is reality. Every human being hurtles day by day toward this, the great defining moment of our existence. In addition, we must humble ourselves to accept the reality of final judgment. God engineered the gospel to reverse the effect of the fall. He engineered it to produce humility. Therefore, Paul told Felix the truth. We saw in the previous chapter that Paul usually began with the wrath of God. Romans chapter 2 indicates that he next moved to the final judgment. (In the case of Felix and the Areopagus, he began here.)

The Bible's description of the day of judgment is sobering: "He comes to judge the earth. He will judge the world in righteousness, and the peoples in his faithfulness" (Ps. 96:13). At the beginning of the twentieth century, the English theologian P. T. Forsyth wrote, "The question of judgment is where all other questions end. It is the central question in religion. How shall I stand before my judge? . . . The question is not about our views; nor is it about our subjective state—how do I feel? But our objective religion—how do I stand?"[2]

The existence of judgment should not surprise us. Daily life confronts us with regular judgments. We judge and we are the subject of judgments. We do this because God made us in his image, and God is a Judge. People are passionate about justice. We have centers for social justice on our college campuses. People want to be treated fairly, and they want friends and family to be treated fairly. We are this way because God is passionate about justice. Our passion for justice has its source in his infinite justice.

When an employer reviews an employee, a judgment occurs. Someone with authority to distribute reward or punishment appraises the employee's performance. Application to an elite college invites judgment. A person in authority measures our grades, test scores, and extracurricular activities against a standard. A judgment is made. We obtain admittance or face rejection.

Judgments start at an early age. I remember turning out for my junior high basketball team. Forty other boys turned out. On the first day the coach told us that only fifteen would make the final cut. The day came. The coach posted the fifteen names, and mine was not there. I was brokenhearted. It took several weeks to recover. Yet my disappointing failure to make the team was insignificant compared with God's final judgment.

Because the consequences are so momentous, few are willing to think hard about the final judgment—eternal conscious torment or unending "joy that is inexpressible and filled with glory" (1 Peter 1:8).

If the Bible is true, however, judgment is inevitable. "We must all appear before the judgment seat of Christ" (2 Cor. 5:10). We often joke that life contains two inevitable events, taxes and death. Actually, there are three—taxes, death, and the final judgment. Every knee will bow to Christ (Phil. 2:10). This means that each person reading these words will someday stand before Christ for judgment. There are no exceptions. We will account for our every thought, motive, and deed. If this is true, and it is, we should live every waking moment with one eye on the judgment to come. This is how spiritually healthy Christians live. In addition, the final judgment should be fundamental and foundational to our witnessing, counseling, and preaching. Success or failure in the presentation of the fact of final judgment is not our responsibility. Our responsibility is to explain it clearly. The results belong to God.

Tony was dying of cancer. Soon he would die and stand before Christ his Judge. Although his wife was a believer, Tony was not. She asked me to share the gospel with him. We met, and after some pleasantries I asked his permission to explain the gospel. He agreed. I explained that God is holy. He listened carefully. I explained that we are not. He still listened. I then explained that after death comes judgment. Then I carefully explained that God's righteousness, his moral perfections revealed in the Ten Commandments, would be the standard by which Tony would be judged. When I mentioned the judgment, he looked at me, snorted in disgust, and said, "I don't believe that!" He died a month later, and I do not know whether he ever came to saving faith.

Another occasion, however, yielded better results. Jeremy, a young man in his early twenties, came to me for counsel. He had grown up in a Christian home. He understood the good news. Yet he had some personal problems. Most importantly, he had never really heard the bad news. That is why he was apathetic, unmotivated, and uninterested in Christianity. In order to check his spiritual pulse, I asked him to explain the gospel. He said something like this: "I believe that God loves me, and I know he has a wonderful plan for my life. When I asked Jesus into my heart, he became my personal Savior."

"Do you mind if we explore the gospel in more detail?" I asked.

"No, I don't mind."

"God does love you. In fact, he loves you much more than you think. But the gospel is bigger than love. You and I have a problem. God is holy in a way that we cannot understand. His standards are perfection. By contrast, you and I are not holy. We are sinners. God is angry with us. After death we will stand before this holy God who is angry. He will judge our every thought, word, and deed. God does not grade on the curve. You must be perfect to pass through his judgment. You have a problem."

By this time Jeremy was leaning forward in his seat, his eyes dilated as if he were on drugs, listening very intently.

Then I added, "That is why the gospel is called 'good news.' It solves this problem. God doesn't want to be angry with you. He wants peace. He wants to be your friend. To accomplish this, he sent his Son on a rescue mission. He came to earth and lived a perfect life. When a person believes the gospel, Christ's perfections are imputed to him; that person's sins are imputed to Christ. Jesus went to the cross to be punished for your sins. God the Father poured out his wrath on his Son instead of on you. That is how much God loves you. On the day of judgment, those who believe will be judged for Christ's works, not their own, and they will pass directly into heaven."

As I shared all of this, a miracle occurred. God opened Jeremy's eyes. He just looked at me and said, "Wow!" God was at work. In that instant God transferred him from death to life. That was several years ago. Jeremy has been faithfully following Christ ever since.

In both of these examples, the reality of the final judgment was a crucial and decisive dimension of the bad news.

JUDGMENT IN ROMANS 2

One of the fundamental ideas in Romans 2 is that the same God who is angry with us will be our judge. "You are storing up wrath for yourself on the day of wrath when God's righteous judgment will be revealed" (Rom. 2:5). This truth should terrify us. Paul wants us to see it and be shaken. Our daily hypocrisy is building up an ever-growing tidal wave of wrath. Today, God restrains his anger, but on the final day it will be released, and its pent-up energy will utterly overwhelm everyone outside of Christ.

Paul wants the members of the Roman church to be clear about one thing: they will be judged according to their works:

> He will render to each one according to his works: to those who by patience in well-doing seek for glory and honor and immortality, he will give eternal life; but for those who are self-seeking and do not obey the truth, but obey unrighteousness, there will be wrath and fury. There will be tribulation and distress for every human being who does evil, the Jew first and also the Greek, but glory and honor and peace for everyone who does good, the Jew first and also the Greek. For God shows no partiality. (Rom. 2:6–11)

Paul is not saying that on the day of judgment we will be saved by our works. Rather, this paragraph casts a hypothetical scene.

To emphasize that God will judge according to our works, Paul asks: what if someone existed who sought God with all his heart and lived righteously? Paul concludes that the person's works would save him. But later, in the third chapter, Paul makes it clear that, short of Christ, this person does not exist. He reminds us that "no one seeks for God" (Rom. 3:11) and that "none is righteous, no, not one" (3:10).

God's judgment will be according to works, and it will also be impartial. It will not help to be a Jew, a member of a certain Christian organization, or the child of a well-known Christian. The basis of God's judgment will be the same for everyone. "God shows no partiality" (Rom. 2:11).

In addition, ignorance will not help. "It is not the hearers of the law . . . but the doers of the law who will be justified" (Rom. 2:13). What about the secular unbeliever and the tribal member in the deep jungles of the Philippines? They don't know God or his law. Surely ignorance will be an excuse. About this person Paul writes that "the work of the law is written on their hearts, while their conscience also bears witness . . . on that day when . . . God judges the secrets of men by Christ Jesus" (2:15–16).

Paul labors to convince us that ultimately no one is ignorant. God has written his law on every human heart. We all intuitively know right from wrong. Jesus reduced the Ten Commandments to two. The first summarizes the first table of the law: love God with your whole heart, soul, mind, and strength. The second summarizes the second table: love your neighbor as yourself (Mark 12:29–31). Paul's point is that everyone enters the world with these two laws engraved on his heart. If God exists, we know we are to love him wholeheartedly. Earlier Paul stressed that everyone is responsible to discern the existence and reality of God from creation (Rom. 1:20). We also know that we should treat others as we want to be treated. Therefore, on the day of judgment everyone who did not obey these two laws will be "without excuse."

It is this fact, God's law written on the human heart, and the universal inward testimony of conscience to its existence, that encouraged Paul to preach the bad news. Because he knew it was there, he aimed his preaching at each man's conscience. The consciences of many of his hearers were hardened and seared by disobedience, or they were encrusted by human traditions. But knowing it was latent in every human heart, Paul addressed himself to the law written on each man's heart and the conscience that bears witness to it. He preached the wrath of God and the judgment to come, trusting the Holy Spirit to raise the conscience from the dead. This is what Paul had in mind when he wrote to the Corinthians that he commended himself "to everyone's conscience in the sight of God" (2 Cor. 4:2). When he preached to Felix about the final judgment, that was his goal.

JUDGMENT IN THE REST OF THE BIBLE

We are in desperate need of this message and Paul's faith in God's power. "Belief in an afterlife remains high in most parts of the world," observes Bruce Milne, "but there is much less willingness today to envisage the post-mortem experience in traditional Christian terms. The thought of a final judgment leading to an eternal destiny in either heaven or hell is widely dismissed."[3]

For this reason, we should note that this teaching is not just Paul's. The final judgment has a substantial history. In fact, Paul's most important sources were the Old Testament and the Gospels. These documents speak emphatically about the final judgment. First, we learn about rivers of fire:

> Our God comes; he does not keep silence;
>   before him is a devouring fire,
>   around him a mighty tempest.

90

HUMBLED BY FINAL JUDGMENT

He calls to the heavens above
    and to the earth, that he may judge his people:
"Gather to me my faithful ones,
    who made a covenant with me by sacrifice!"
The heavens declare his righteousness,
    for God himself is judge! (Ps. 50:3–6)

Psalm 97:3 supports Psalm 50:

Fire goes before him
    and burns up his adversaries all around.

The prophet Daniel adds significant details:

As I looked,

thrones were placed,
    and the Ancient of Days took his seat;
. . . .
his throne was fiery flames;
    its wheels were burning fire. (Dan. 7:9)

With these texts in mind, Paul writes:

When the Lord Jesus is revealed from heaven with his mighty angels in flaming fire, [he will inflict] vengeance on those who do not know God and on those who do not obey the gospel of our Lord Jesus. (2 Thess. 1:7–8)

The Holy Spirit has designed these texts to disturb us, to arrest our attention, to humble us, to make us pause and think hard. Every time I read them, I think of the films of World War II GIs blasting recalcitrant Japanese soldiers out of concrete pillboxes with flamethrowers. It is not a pleasant picture. In fact, the reality that these texts depict is much worse.

This is the same God who made the sun. Temperatures there approach 6,000 degrees centigrade. The sun is immense. It would take a million earths to fill it. The God who made this medium-sized star is the One who promises to bring fire with him when he comes in judgment. Like the psalmist, we should respond, "What is man that you are mindful of him . . . ?" (Ps. 8:4).

The Bible adds that this judgment will not be private. All our sins, known and secret, will be made public. Everyone will know how we treated our spouse and children in the secret confines of our home. Everyone will know about our hidden sexual sins. Our good deeds will also be made public. "For nothing is hidden that will not be made manifest," Jesus repeatedly told his disciples. "Nor is anything secret that will not be known and come to light" (Luke 8:17). When will this happen? At the final judgment. "But the day of the Lord will come like a thief," wrote Peter, "and then the heavens will pass away with a roar, and the heavenly bodies will be burned up and dissolved, and the earth and the works that are done on it will be exposed" (2 Peter 3:10).

In addition, Christ will be our Judge: "on that day . . . [when] according to my gospel, God judges the secrets of men by Christ Jesus" (Rom. 2:16). Jesus repeatedly described himself as our future Judge:

> When the Son of Man comes in his glory, and all the angels with him, then he will sit on his glorious throne. Before him will be gathered all the nations, and he will separate people one from another as a shepherd separates the sheep from the goats. (Matt. 25:31–32)

God the Son is the Judge because he died for us and lived among us. On that day, unbelievers will stand before the One whose dying sacrifice they rejected, the One before whom they would not humble themselves to receive mercy. Now they will call "to the mountains and rocks, 'Fall on us and hide us from the face of him who is seated on the throne, and from the wrath of the Lamb, for the great day of their wrath has come, and who can stand?'" (Rev. 6:16–17).

By contrast, believers will be judged by Christ, their Friend, the One who died for them, the One who reconciled them to his Father at the cost of his blood, the One who loves them with tenderness, compassion, and mercy, and the One who intercedes for them day and night. They will rejoice that they humbled themselves, embraced the gospel, and now look forward to an eternity with the God-man who loved them and gave his life for them.

It is also important to note that no one will complain that Christ was unfair. Rather, "every knee [will] bow . . . and every tongue confess that Jesus Christ is Lord, to the glory of God the Father" (Phil. 2:10–11). As difficult as this sounds, all men will acknowledge the righteousness, the fairness of God's judgments, even those now consigned to hell forever. In fact, the perfections of God's judgments will be one reason for our eternal joy and praise.

DISTRIBUTIVE JUDGMENT

God's justice is "distributive." This means that punishment or reward follows his judgments. "Retribution," observes Dr. J. I. Packer, "is the inescapable moral law of creation; God will see that each person sooner or later receives what he deserves—if not here, then hereafter. This is one of the basic facts of life. And, being made in God's image, we all know in our hearts that this is *right*. This is how it ought to be."[4]

Jesus repeatedly warned us that his judgment would terminate in one of two destinations—hell or heaven. In fact,

Jesus warned of hell more often than any other person in Scripture. He did this because hell is real. He did it to get people's attention—to turn their thoughts to God and eternal things.

What makes hell so horrible is its eternality, and this fact the Bible is not shy to stress. John the Baptist warned that God would burn the impenitent "with *unquenchable* fire" (Matt. 3:12). Jesus said the wicked would be cast into the "*eternal* fire prepared for the devil and his angels" (25:41). He also promised that after the judgment the goats would go away into "*eternal* punishment," but the sheep into "*eternal* life" (25:46). Jonathan Edwards observed that it is the eternality of hell that makes it so horrible. You could bear it for ten thousand years. It would be difficult, but hope would sustain you. There would be an end in sight. But what makes eternal conscious punishment so horrible is the utter despair in the word *eternal*.[5]

In order to humble them, effective preachers drive their listeners by hell on the way to heaven. This was the method of the aforementioned Edward Payson (1790–1830). About the eternality of hell, in words foreign to the modern world, he preached, "The fire of his anger must burn forever. It is a fire, which cannot be quenched, unless God should change or cease to exist. It is this, which constitutes the most terrible ingredient of that cup, which impenitent sinners must drink."[6]

The first objection to hell is that it seems unfair. Eternal conscious torment for normal, daily, human mistakes and blunders? Come on. Certainly God is more tolerant than that. Can't he endure a little weakness? But that is the point. His justice is inflexible. Were he to relax his justice for one moment, God would not be the perfect Being described in Scripture, and the whole universe would unravel.

Most people who think hard about eternal realities object to hell not because they don't believe in justice. They object to hell because they are proud. They don't think their sins are really that serious. Eternal conscious torment is an injustice. It feels too severe. We don't see the correlation between the horrors of sin and the horrors of hell.

For example, we don't object to the biblical teaching about hell when we see a correlation between a person's moral character and hell. In their book *Mao*,[7] the biography of Mao Tse-tung (1893–1976), the authors estimate that Mao murdered approximately 80 million fellow Chinese. Most were tortured to death in gruesome, hideous ways. These deaths were not acts of war. They were punishment for perceived rebellion, petty offenses, or just being in the wrong place at the wrong time. He slaughtered men, women, and children indiscriminately— even close family members. We look at a monster like Mao and think: *Eternal conscious torment? Yep! It is appropriate. The punishment fits the crime.*

If this is true, we don't really have a problem with justice terminating in hell. Our problem is pride. We are arrogant. We don't think our sins are really that bad. As we will see in the next chapter, however, our sins are *infinitely* offensive to God, so there is a perfect proportion or correlation between what seem to be our "petty" sins and a punishment of infinite duration.

There is an irony here. The more people believe in hell, the more apt they are to create heaven on earth. And the less people believe in hell, the more apt they are to turn this world into the very hell they deny. None of the monster-dictators of the twentieth century—Mao (China), Joseph Stalin (Russia), Adolf Hitler (Germany), Idi Amin (Uganda), or Pol Pot (Cambodia)—believed in the life to come, let alone hell. Because their pride was completely unchecked by fear of eternal accounting, they created the closest thing to hell on earth that history has to date witnessed.

God's justice doesn't just distribute punishment; it also distributes reward—what the Bible calls *heaven*. For those who believe the gospel, this is wonderful news. God rewards believers with the reward that his Son deserves, and they get it at Christ's expense. This is astounding. Christ was perfect. He was sinless. He obeyed his Father even to the point of death on a cross. God imputes these perfections to those who believe the gospel. Then God rewards them for eternity with the love, peace, joy, and happiness that Christ's sinless perfections deserve.

There are two guarantees that God will fulfill his promise to distribute reward to the saints. The first is God's justice. We have noted that God must be just, that his justice is utterly inflexible, and that the universe would implode if God acted unjustly. This is our first guarantee. God must reward the believer. We are clothed in Christ's deeds, and God must reward us accordingly. The very justice that stands against the unbeliever has become the believer's ally. And the second guarantee is God's love. He loves us. The measure of his love is the death of his Son at Calvary.

Like hell, heaven is eternal. Just as the eternality of hell is what makes it so horrible, the eternality of heaven is what makes it so wonderful. Once in heaven, you cannot be removed. The reward is eternal and unbreakable. It cannot be lost. This means utter hope, the complete absence of despair, the elimination of all fear of rejection.

Heaven is a place, but not an ethereal place with saints floating on clouds plucking harps. Heaven will be a renovated, re-created earth, an earth without sin or the possibility of sin, a world where all sinners and causes of sin have been consigned to hell forever. In the words of the apostle Peter, "But according to his promise we are waiting for new heavens and a new earth in which righteousness dwells" (2 Peter 3:13).

Finally, and most importantly, heaven is a person. It is not the presence of deceased relatives that makes heaven so wonderful. It is Christ that makes heaven wonderful. Heaven without Christ would be just another place. What makes heaven heavenly is the presence of God in all his radiant glory. Heaven is wherever Christ is. This is how the book of Revelation describes our final reward:

> The throne of God and of the Lamb will be in it, and his servants will worship him. They will see his face, and his name will be on their foreheads. (Rev. 22:3–4)

THE CROSS AND JUDGMENT

It is impossible to see the cross of Christ and not possess a strong conviction about the final judgment. If the cross is anything, it is an expression of both God's love and his justice. This theme begins in Exodus and culminates at the cross.

Exodus 34:6 is one of those passages around which much of the Bible turns. Moses wanted to know God. He wanted to see into the divine nature, so he asked to see God's glory. Reminding Moses that no one can see him and live, God said no! Instead, God agreed to *declare* his glory to Moses. He hid Moses in a rock and passed by, announcing:

> The LORD, the LORD, a God merciful and gracious, slow to anger, and abounding in steadfast love and faithfulness, keeping steadfast love for thousands, forgiving iniquity and transgression and sin, but who will by no means clear the guilty, visiting the iniquity of the fathers on the children and the children's children, to the third and the fourth generation. (Ex. 34:6–7)

The careful reader will notice an apparent inconsistency in this passage. First, God declares his grace, mercy, and longing to forgive. "A God merciful and gracious, slow to anger . . . forgiving iniquity and transgression and sin." But then he turns and promises that he will not "clear the guilty, visiting

97

the iniquity of the fathers on the children and the children's children." In other words, at the heart of God's glory are two passions—love and justice. Both must be expressed, and neither can ever be compromised. Justice is mandatory. God owes his creatures justice. But God's love is voluntary. God loves his creatures, but not because we have a claim on it, not because we merit it.

This text must have puzzled the Old Testament saints. They had no way to understand this apparent inconsistency. But New Testament believers have the cross. The cross paints a picture of Exodus 34:6. First, the cross shows us that God is "merciful and gracious, slow to anger, and abounding in steadfast love and faithfulness." None of us have a problem here. From childhood we have been taught that "God is love." It is God's justice or judgment that surprises us. The cross was the greatest demonstration of God's inflexible passion for justice in history. It illustrates verse 7, "who will by no means clear the guilty." When Jesus bore our sin on the cross, God judged him with the judgment that our sin deserved—crucifixion. Chapter 3 has already described the horrors of crucifixion. Paul tells us that Jesus went to the cross so that God could be both "just and the justifier of the one who has faith in Jesus" (Rom. 3:26). God designed the cross to display both a passion to forgive and a passion for justice. At the cross God fully punished our sins. He satisfied the demands of his justice. He did this so that he could lavish all who believe with unmerited grace, mercy, and love.

As we see the justice displayed by the cross, we become absolutely convinced that a day of final judgment is coming. How can a Being who loves justice this intensely and inflexibly fail to punish the sin of those who do not believe?

The cross reminds us that there are only two kinds of people—those who let Jesus absorb God's justice for them, and those who take it themselves for eternity in hell. "Do you want to see the greatest evidence of the love of God?" asks D. A. Carson. "Go to the cross. Do you want to see the greatest evidence of the justice of God? Go to the cross. It is where wrath and mercy meet. Holiness and peace kiss each other. The climax of redemptive history is the cross."[8]

THE BENEFITS OF PREACHING JUDGMENT

Many benefits accrue to those who meditate on the final judgment. The majority of non-Christians, and sadly a large number in our pews, assume that God will judge on the curve. In other words, if I am as good as most, I will get in. Pride is the foundation of this conviction. By contrast, the reality that this chapter has described motivates humility. We cannot pass through the final judgment on personal merit or by being as good as the average person. The day of final judgment exposes our great personal need. We are bankrupt. God's standards humble us. They force us to rest in Christ's merits, not our own.

The doctrine of final judgment also keeps us focused on eternal things. It encourages us to "seek the things that are above" (Col. 3:1). It helps us to die to earthly mindedness. It puts the brevity of life in perspective. "It is appointed for man to die once, and after that comes judgment" (Heb. 9:27). To those who believe this, and believe the gospel, peace with God and life is the result. How important are our daily trials and stresses? A final judgment approaches. On that day we will see these small issues in their true perspective.

The doctrine of final judgment also points us to the love and grace of God. Because God loves us and sent his Son to live a perfect life in our place, Christ, our Judge, will declare us "justified." He came to bear the wrath that would have otherwise been directed at us. He came to make us God's friends. God has done what we could never do. At the expense of his

Son, an infinite cost to himself, he has prepared us for the final judgment. Why? "Love . . . that surpasses knowledge" (Eph. 3:19) motivated him.

The doctrine of final judgment keeps us zealous. We saw in the previous chapter that people who do not feel their need are usually lukewarm. By contrast, the reality of final judgment keeps our personal need front and center. It causes us to abound with thanksgiving (Col. 2:7). We know what we deserve, but we are not going to get it!

The doctrine of final judgment also motivates us to go out to the lost. Their condition is hopeless. It also motivates conversions. When God impresses an unbeliever with the certainty of judgment, he turns to God for justification.

Finally, this crucial subject motivates parenting. Someday our children will stand before the judgment seat of Christ. Men and women who are sensitive to this truth make the best parents. It heightens their earnestness and their attentiveness to their parental duties.

We can sum it all up by saying that when the final judgment is not a regular fixture of our counseling, preaching, and evangelizing, Christians tend toward spiritual sluggishness, apathy, and earthly mindedness.

SUMMARY

Judgment is where Paul began when he spoke to the Areopagus. Judgment is where he began with Felix. Judgment was fundamental to his gospel proclamation: "Him we proclaim, *warning* everyone and teaching everyone with all wisdom" (Col. 1:28).

The reality of the final judgment is deeply humbling. God's justice is inflexible. It is distributive. Christ will be our Judge. He will judge us on the basis of our deeds, and the standard will be perfection. Sin is infinitely serious. It deserves eternal damnation. If this is true, unbelievers have a problem. (Chapter 6 will discuss the glorious solution.)

I was a law student for one year. My grade for the entire year's work was based on one exam in each class at the end of the year. Papers, quizzes, and homework contributed nothing to my final grade. The entire year's work rested on that one exam. The pressure was tremendous. I spent the entire year thinking about, preparing for, and hoping that I would do well on that exam. My answers would be judged by my professors, and I would be graded accordingly.

If the outcome of the final judgment is infinitely more important than an academic grade, why is this subject so seldom discussed in the contemporary church? Something is broken. Certainly Paul felt its relevance. To Christians, not unbelievers, he wrote, "For we must all appear before the judgment seat of Christ." Why? "So that each one may receive what is due for what he has done in the body, whether good or evil" (2 Cor. 5:10). Paul believed the gospel. He believed that God would justify him on the last day. Nevertheless, he continued: "Knowing the fear of the Lord, we persuade others" (2 Cor. 5:11).

Why would one confident of his future justification fear God? The answer is simple. God had commanded Paul to take the gospel to the Gentiles. He feared that he would have to stand before God on that final day and confess that he had not "persuaded" the Gentiles as God had commanded him. The words of Paul Barnett on this passage are insightful:

> It is not therefore condemnation that he fears (for there is none in Christ), but evaluation. It is not the loss of salvation—for it cannot be lost—but the loss of commendation which is at stake. . . . God's gift to Paul was to be an apostle; the gospel was entrusted to him. One day he would stand before the Lord to give an account of his faithfulness as a missionary. Whatever our ministry from God, it is sobering

to note that what each one of us has done will one day be made manifest at the judgment seat of Christ.[9]

Paul began his gospel with the bad news. He explained it in the first three chapters of Romans. Paul devoted over 1,200 words to the bad news but only 188 words to the good news. Why? He knew that man's basic sin is pride and that God had sent the gospel to humble us. He also knew that no one enters God's kingdom until his faith has begun to humble him. Chapter 4 devoted itself to the first leg of that humbling journey—the wrath of God. This chapter dealt with the second leg—the final judgment.

This teaching humbles us. *I am in trouble. The day of judgment is approaching. I cannot meet God's standards. It will be heaven or hell. There is no third option. What will I do?* This humbling was the intended effect of Paul's preaching. As Richard Baxter (1615–91) wrote, "The very design of the gospel is to abase us; and the work of grace is begun and carried on in humiliation. Humility is not a mere ornament of a Christian, but an essential part of the new creature. It is a contradiction in terms, to be a Christian, and not be humble."[10]

The third leg of the bad news is the sinfulness of sin, and that is the subject of chapter 5.

5

Humbled by the Sinfulness of Sin

The Biblical gospel asserts . . . that the self is twisted, that it is maladjusted in its relationship to God and others, that it is full of deceit and rationalizations, that it is lawless, that it is in rebellion, and indeed one must die to self in order to live.

—David F. Wells[1]

NO ONE CAN BE USED by God to help others grow in humility until he has come face-to-face with the biblical doctrine of sin. I recently overheard a Christian say, "No matter how badly you think of yourself, no matter how guilty you feel, no matter how deep your sense of moral bankruptcy and failure, you have not yet seen the depth of your sin. It is always worse than you think." That was Dr. William Plumer's point in the nineteenth century: "The truth is, no man ever thought himself a greater sinner before God than he really

103

was. Nor was any man ever more distressed at his sins than he had just cause to be."[2]

Generally, this is not how the church sees sin at the beginning of the twenty-first century. D. A. Carson, professor at Trinity Evangelical Divinity School, has been conducting missions on college campuses since the 1970s. "The hardest truth to get across to [university students]," he writes, "is not the existence of God, the Trinity, the deity of Christ, Jesus' substitutionary atonement, or Jesus' resurrection. . . . No, the hardest truth to get across to this generation is what the Bible says about sin."[3] Students are resistant to this teaching because they are proud. From infancy they have been taught that they are inherently good and wonderful. The therapeutic movement has evangelized them.

How do we change this mind-set? After all is said and done, all defective views of sin can be traced to unbelief or ignorance. We just don't believe the Bible, or we don't know what it says. "In all unbelief there are these two things," noted Horatius Bonar (1808–89), "a good opinion of one's self, and a bad opinion of God."[4]

Bonar's words sound foreign to the modern ear for several reasons. Either we have never been taught about sin (common today) or we have been taught about it, but do not *want* to believe it. It is a humbling subject. It is an unpleasant subject. Most obituaries don't use the words *death, dying,* or *died.* They talk about *passing away. Sin* is the same kind of word. We make "unfortunate decisions," "errors in judgment," or "unwise choices," but "sin" is outside of our cultural norms. As we noted in the first two chapters, however, until we come face-to-face with sin there will be little humility, few conversions, and only modest changes in our character. Our joy, our security in God's love, and our desire to love others will also be diminished.

We begin our discussion of sin not with sin itself, but with the holiness of God. We can't understand sin by comparing ourselves with each other. We can understand sin only by comparing self with an absolute, infinite standard of holiness—God himself.

GOD IS HOLY

God has many attributes, but the most important is his holiness. God is holy. He is utterly intolerant of evil. He cannot even look upon it. This is not the street view of God. Many see him (or her) as a tolerant grandfatherly figure winking at sin from a celestial rocking chair. But the prophet Habakkuk, who knew God well, wrote, "You . . . are of purer eyes than to see evil and cannot look at wrong" (Hab. 1:13). Because God is holy, he hates evil. We discussed this truth in a previous chapter. Not only does he hate evil, but he also hates good deeds done for the wrong motive. Even our "righteous deeds are like a filthy garment" in God's sight (Isa. 64:6 NASB). The Hebrew for "filthy garment" is a strong word. It implies a soiled, smelly cloth, for example, a soiled menstrual cloth.[5]

My grandchildren paid us a visit on a hot summer weekend. When they left on Sunday night, our garbage can was filled with soiled diapers. Monday continued hot. Late Tuesday afternoon, I opened the garage door and a stench greeted me that was almost unbearable. With my right hand I plugged my nose. With my left hand I picked up the garbage can and removed it far from the house to await garbage pickup.

Isaiah 64:6 implies that this is how God sees not our bad deeds, but our *good* deeds when disconnected from faith in the gospel. They are like "filthy" or "polluted" garments. My garbage smelled bad, but can you imagine what Isaiah's "polluted garments" smelled like in a hot Middle Eastern climate twenty-seven hundred years ago? If this is how God feels about our *good* deeds, how does he feel about our sins?

God's holiness, expressed as moral purity, is beyond human comprehension. "Can mortal man be in the right before God?"

asks Job. "Can a man be pure before his Maker? Even in his servants he puts no trust, and his *angels* he charges with error" (Job 4:17–18). A few chapters later, Job continues:

> How then can man be in the right before God?
>   How can he who is born of woman be pure?
> Behold, even the moon is not bright,
>   and the stars are not pure in his eyes;
> how much less man, who is a maggot,
>   and the son of man, who is a worm! (Job 25:4–6)

If inanimate objects with no capacity to rebel—the moon and stars—are not pure in his eyes, what hope is there for you and me? Job even calls us "worms." Three is the biblical number for emphasis. Scripture uses this language exactly two other times to describe us, making a total of three.[6] Yes, God made us in his image and likeness, and for this we are deeply grateful. We are fearfully and wonderfully made. Nevertheless, Job's words describe what sin has done to tarnish the image and likeness.

This is why, when Moses asked to see God's glory, the Almighty responded, "You cannot see my face, for man shall not see me and live" (Ex. 33:20). Man is so defiled by sin that, to uphold his integrity, God would have to destroy us rather than allow us, in our fallen condition, to behold his essential, unveiled glory.

Even the sinless seraphim continuously worship day and night, crying out, "Holy, holy, holy." Despite their moral purity, they dare not gaze upon God. With two wings they respectfully cover their eyes. With two more they cover their feet, for his presence makes even the very ground about him holy. And with the remaining two they fly. What kind of moral purity requires even sinless, adoring creatures to veil their eyes and cover their feet in worship?

These passages, and a host of others, state the problem simply: God is holy. We are ill-equipped to comprehend it.

Our sinful nature opens a massive gulf between us and God. It is like the gorge that separates the rims of the Grand Canyon. In places it is several miles across. This chasm cannot be bridged with human effort. You can't jump from one side to the other. That is what sin does to our relationship with God. It forges an abyss that cannot be bridged with human effort or good intentions.

In addition, sin is comprehensive. It affects our entire being—intellect, will, emotions, and body. It alienates us from God, it alienates us from our self, and it alienates us from our fellow man. It affects everything that matters.

As long as our standard is other people, we will never understand sin. Sin makes little sense until we come face-to-face with the holiness of God.

HOW GOD SEES SIN

Redemptive history shows us how God sees sin. For stealing a piece of fruit God judged Adam and all his descendants with sin and death. The fruits of this judgment are pride, rebellion, death, war, poverty, starvation, social injustice, cancer, heart disease, aging, death, and political and social oppression. And what was the sin that produced all this? Was it adultery, or murder, or incest, or homosexuality, or some other especially grievous sin? No! It was the simple sin of taking some forbidden fruit. We saw in the previous chapter that God is infinitely just. His punishments are always commensurate with the crime. This means that all the suffering unleashed by sin was God's righteous judgment for one theft of fruit. This puts sin in perspective. We think little of our petty lusts, condescending looks, selfish thoughts, and minor idolatries, but they are profoundly heinous in God's sight.

So we come to Romans chapter 3. Paul wants his readers to grapple with all of this, and in the process be humbled. He began the good news with Romans 1, the wrath of God. Then, in chapter 2, he moved to the final judgment. Christ will judge each of us on the basis of our works. Now, in Romans 3:9–18, he gives us a God's-eye view of sin.

> For we have already charged that all, both Jews and Greeks, are under sin, as it is written:
>
> "None is righteous, no, not one;
>> no one understands;
>> no one seeks for God.
> All have turned aside; together they have become worthless;
>> no one does good,
>> not even one."
> "Their throat is an open grave;
>> they use their tongues to deceive."
> "The venom of asps is under their lips."
>> "Their mouth is full of curses and bitterness."
> "Their feet are swift to shed blood;
>> in their paths are ruin and misery,
> and the way of peace they have not known."
>> "There is no fear of God before their eyes."
>> (Rom. 3:9–18, quoting Pss. 14:1–3 and 53:1–3;
>> 5:9; 140:3; 10:7; Prov. 1:16; Ps. 36:1)

This statement is comprehensive. First, Paul makes the point that all men are sinners. Then he shows us how sin has defiled six facets of the human personality—our understanding, our desires, our behavior, our speech, our relationships with people, and our relationship with God. Sin has defiled them all.

SIN IS COMPREHENSIVE

First, sin affects all men. None are excepted. "All, both Jews and Greeks, are under sin" (Rom. 3:9). From God's perspective, humanity divides into two classes—Jews and Greeks (non-Jews). God wants us to know that, with the exception of Jesus Christ, both classes enter the world bound by sin. Self is at the center of our universe. We lack faith in God. We are dead in our trespasses and sins, and are by nature children of wrath (Eph. 2:1–3). Our number-one concern is *me* and *mine.* We actively suppress the knowledge of God (Rom. 1:18). When confronted, our first response is self-justification. We make our own rules and run our own lives—and, by doing so, declare ourselves the god of our personal existence. This self-worship is the worst form of idolatry.

All are under the power of sin. Stated another way, "None is righteous, no, not one" (Rom. 3:10). Righteousness is the essential quality that we must have to be acceptable to God. Righteousness makes us not guilty in God's sight. Without it, we will be alienated from God for eternity.

But verse 10 tells us that no one has righteousness. We are born without it. We can't earn it. We can't "mature" our way into it. We can't earn it by trying a little harder. Mother Teresa didn't have it. Not even Paul had it. "None is righteous"! This is a serious problem. In fact, our lack of righteousness is life's one really great problem, a problem beside which all others are trivial.

Not only does sin affect all men, but it also affects all men comprehensively. It affects every facet of our personality. The rest of this chapter will describe the six expressions of unrighteousness that we have already mentioned.

UNRIGHTEOUS UNDERSTANDING

First, sin distorts and twists our understanding. "No one understands" (Rom. 3:11). Sin cripples our thinking. It darkens our minds. "They are darkened in their understanding," Paul wrote, "alienated from the life of God because of the ignorance that is in them, due to their hardness of heart" (Eph. 4:18).

Sin shrouds our thoughts in mental darkness, rendering true belief in God humanly impossible. It severs our capacity to simultaneously understand God and *love* him for who he is. "No one understands" doesn't mean that the fallen mind can't learn theology. It means that without regeneration, we might detest what we learn about God. At best, we will be completely unaffected by it. A seminary professor can dissect the Bible, but without the Holy Spirit's illumination, he can't love God for who he is.

This lack of understanding is what the Bible means when it says that God is the One who hides himself (Isa. 6:8–10). We are sinners. Our minds are darkened. We can know God only to the degree that he unveils himself. The initiative is with God. "Man's understanding is so darkened that he can see nothing of God in God," writes Dr. Plumer, "nothing of holiness in holiness, nothing of good in good, nothing of evil in evil, nor anything of sinfulness in sin. Nay, it is so darkened that he fancies himself to see good in evil, and evil in good, happiness in sin, and misery in holiness."[7]

We all understand the god we have invented in our imagination, but that is because he is a made-up god. He does not threaten us. We have created him in our fallen, sinful image. Therefore, he presents us with none of the conundrums of infinity. He is not the God of wrath and justice described by Paul in the first and second chapters of Romans. We are comfortable with him. We assume that he (or maybe she) is tolerant of sin and sinners. We picture him as being open to new and different ideas. He judges no one and condemns no one.

He is the antithesis of the God of the Bible.

No one would invent the God of the Bible. He is an infinitely holy deity who, in our sinful condition, stands implacably against us even as he loves us by dying for us. Invented gods are in the image of their maker. Like their creator, they are simple. A Christian, however, embraces the biblical God and loves him for who he is.

But sin doesn't affect just the understanding. It also perverts and misdirects our desires.

UNRIGHTEOUS DESIRES

Second, our desires—the thrust of our lives, our goals—are also unrighteousness. "No one seeks for God. All have turned aside; together they have become worthless" (Rom. 3:11–12). We seek our happiness, but we don't seek God. We seek self-actualization, glory, or comfort, but we don't seek God sufficiently to earn his favor.

Some object, "What about the non-Christians who sincerely seek God but don't find him? Surely God will show them mercy at the final judgment." But Paul is clear. No one seeks God with sufficient sincerity and intensity to merit God's favor. In fact, instead of seeking him, which is our first obligation, verse 12 testifies that we have all "turned aside." To seek God acceptably, one would need to seek God's glory with single-minded, undistracted devotion. This person's motives would be Godward, not manward. He would seek God in order to obey him, suffer for him, and, if need be, die for him. No one can, or will, do this without God's enabling.

Therefore, if anyone seeks God sincerely, it is because God draws that person to himself. That is why Jesus said, "No one knows the Father except the Son and anyone to whom the Son chooses to reveal him" (Matt. 11:27).

Chained by unbelief, darkness, and self-centeredness, we are enslaved by sin, which distorts our desires, goals, and aims. We take great pride in our sincerity, but God's appraisal is different. We have "together . . . become worthless."

Corrupt minds and desires generate corrupt behavior, and that is Paul's next assertion.

UNRIGHTEOUS BEHAVIOR

Third, an unrighteous thought life and unrighteous desires will terminate in unrighteous behavior. Therefore, Romans 3:12 reads, "No one does good, not even one." As we have already noted, three is God's number of emphasis. It is like a divine exclamation point. The Bible repeats this verse exactly three times (see Ps. 14:3; 53:3; and here).

A non-Christian friend asked me to explain what Christians believe. Since I knew that he would feel no need for Christ unless the Word of God humbled him, I started with God's holiness: "God is holy in a way that we cannot understand. He hates evil. One must be perfect to get into heaven. We have a problem. In God's sight, 'No one does good.'"

"Certainly I'm as good as my wife and friends," he objected.

"You're right. When compared to other people, you are better than some and worse than others, but other people are not the standard. God is the standard, and he doesn't grade on a curve. To be 'good' in God's sight, you would need to obey the first commandment—love God with all your heart, soul, mind, and strength—24/7.[8] This is the standard. This is what righteousness looks like." My friend now had an opportunity to humble himself and confess his need.

When Scripture says, "No one does good," it doesn't mean that humans don't do some good deeds, or that we are as bad as we could be. Because God formed men and women in his image, most people regularly do good to others. They care for their children, are faithful to their spouses, obey the law, and pay their bills.

Paul's phrase, "No one does good," does not deny this. Rather, it is making the point that no one does enough good, consistently, to meet God's standards. To be "good" in God's sight, every deed must be informed by faith in God and motivated by a passion for his glory. That is what true virtue looks like. Therefore, even if one invested his entire life in alleviating the suffering of the poor, but the motive did not proceed from faith in God and a passion for the glory of God, it would not be virtue. It would be idolatry. It would be making people and their needs more important than God. This is what "No one does good, not even one" means.

UNRIGHTEOUS SPEECH

Fourth, Paul wants us to know that our hearts are unrighteous. Our speech makes this clear. "Out of the abundance of the *heart*," Jesus said, "the mouth speaks" (Matt. 12:34). Our speech advertises our true heart condition. That is why Paul adds speech to the catalogue of sinful categories:

> "Their throat is an open grave;
>   they use their tongues to deceive.
> The venom of asps is under their lips."
>   "Their mouth is full of curses and bitterness"
>   (Rom. 3:13–14).

You might argue, "Well, I do occasionally speak inappropriately, but surely it isn't all that bad." Again, Paul is not describing how *we* see our speech. He describes how God sees it. Our speech is like a red neon sign, flashing, "The heart is deceitful above all things, and desperately sick; who can understand it?" (Jer. 17:9).

Record your speech for a day and then meditate on what it says about your heart condition. A disloyal heart gossips. A proud heart criticizes. A heart filled with selfish ambition leaks jealousy. A hateful heart slanders. A fearful heart speaks words of anxiety and stress. A heart that fears man avoids confrontation or flatters. An insecure heart boasts. An ambitious heart speaks words of self-promotion. An ungrateful heart grumbles and complains. A proud heart fabricates excuses for its behavior.

That is why, when Isaiah saw the Lord high and lifted up, he responded: "Woe is me! *For I am lost; for I am a man of unclean lips, and I dwell in the midst of a people of unclean lips*" (Isa. 6:5). In an instant, by the power of the Holy Spirit, Isaiah saw the connection between his speech and his heart. He was devastated. We need the same insight, and it should promote the fear of God. "On the day of judgment people will *give account for every careless word they speak,* for by your words you will be justified, and by your words you will be condemned" (Matt. 12:36–37).

Our speech is the window through which God looks to see the condition of our hearts.

UNRIGHTEOUS RELATIONSHIPS WITH PEOPLE

Fifth, our relationships with others are unrighteous. "Their feet are swift to shed blood" (Rom. 3:15). "Well, at least I am okay here," you might be thinking. "I have never shed anyone's blood." But God's concern is the heart. The Jews didn't understand this concept. They thought their actions were God's main concern. Yet Jesus said that the roots of bloodshed are in everyone's hearts:

> You have heard that it was said to those of old, "You shall not murder; and whoever murders will be liable to judgment." But I say to you that everyone who is angry with his brother will be liable to judgment; whoever insults his brother will be liable to the council; and whoever says, "You fool!" will be liable to the hell of fire. (Matt. 5:21–22)

In God's sight, an angry, spiteful, slanderous heart is a heart capable of murder. Although the deed is more serious than the desire, the desire is of the same nature as the deed. The desire, the heart condition, is the real issue. Slander, unwillingness to forgive, and jealousy are all symptoms of a murderous heart, and it is the heart that God sees.

Heart hatred is a spiritual cancer destroying every capacity for lasting peace and happiness. "In their paths are ruin and misery, and the way of peace they have not known" (Rom. 3:16–17). Human history is the story of this verse. It is a record of misery, ruin, and strife. Twice Isaiah warns us, " 'There is no peace,' says the LORD, 'for the wicked' " (Isa. 48:22; 57:21). One historian has testified that only fifty years of recorded history have been without war. The last hundred years alone have seen two world wars that have killed at least 100 million people. Some historians estimate the death toll on World War II's Eastern Front alone, waged between Adolf Hitler and Joseph Stalin, to be over 40 million.[9] The rising divorce rate testifies to once-happy marriages that are now battlegrounds. The United States has more lawyers per capita than any other nation in history. Sin is lethal.

When God says that "their feet are swift to shed blood," this is his perspective, and it is the heart that he sees.

UNRIGHTEOUS RELATIONSHIP WITH GOD

Sixth, our relationship with God is unrighteous. "There is no fear of God before their eyes" (Rom. 3:18). The modern church has little use for the fear of God. *Isn't that Old Testament? Doesn't "perfect love cast out fear"?* (1 John 4:18).

Yes! Perfect love casts out fear, but it is everything *but* the fear of God that it drives out. The fear of God is an essential biblical virtue. In fact, failure to fear God is sin. "And now, Israel, what does the LORD your God *require of you*, but to fear the LORD your God" (Deut. 10:12)—yet few virtues are so scarce in the contemporary church.

The one who fears God feels both his sinfulness and God's holiness. He is growing in humility. In fact, the Bible often depicts the fear of God as synonymous with humility. The one who fears God has begun to overcome the deceitfulness of his proud heart. He has begun to see himself in God's light. In his own eyes he is becoming smaller, while God is growing larger day by day. He sees his moral bankruptcy with increasing clarity. Because of all this, it stands to reason that the fear of God is essential for growth in godliness.

When was the last time you heard a sermon or read a book on the fear of God? When was the last time you discussed it or prayed for it? Why is this subject so studiously avoided in today's church? "The fear of the LORD is a fountain of life" (Prov. 14:27). Why aren't we drinking from this fountain?

Pride diminishes our capacity to fear God. In other words, self-flattery shuts down the fear of God. "Transgression speaks to the wicked deep in his heart," observed David. "There is no fear of God before his eyes. *For he flatters himself in his own eyes* that his iniquity cannot be found out and hated" (Ps. 36:1–2). Pride (self-flattery) quenches the fear of God. And when the fear of God is absent, pride will always fill the vacuum.

So far, this chapter has stressed the holiness of God and the comprehensive sinfulness of humanity. God is infinitely holy. We cannot comprehend the beauty of his holiness. It is a transcendent, blinding-white purity. In addition, sin has affected every aspect of our personality, and God hates sin. If all of this is true, we should expect a massive collision between infinite holiness and human sinfulness. That is exactly what we find.

UNRIGHTEOUS NATURE

The problem is deeper than our actions. Sin also affects our nature—who we are from the moment of conception.

A grove of aspen trees grows next to my lawn. Their roots extend as far as sixty or seventy feet from the mother trees. From these, little aspens sprout in the middle of my grass. At first, I sprayed them with a commercial brush killer. It killed the visible seedling, but did nothing to solve the underlying problem—the sprawling, invisible root system six inches under the surface. Little trees kept sprouting. It became apparent that attacking the visible shoots was a waste. I had to kill the source, the mother trees from which all the runners came.

Sin and sins work the same way. Throughout Paul's letters the little word *sin* (singular) usually refers to who we are by nature. It is the real problem. It is the mother tree extending her roots. By contrast, *sins* (plural) refers to the specific actions. They are the visible seedlings of lying, cheating, slander, gossip, boasting, lust, and rebellion—the behaviors that Paul has just described in Romans 3.

My point is this: The problem is not what we do; it is who we *are*. Even if I committed no *sins*, I would still be condemned. Why? My nature, inherited from Adam, is abhorrent to God. We are "*by nature* children of wrath, like the rest of mankind" (Eph. 2:3). Even while we are fast asleep, doing nothing right or wrong, sin makes us noxious to God. *Original sin* is the theological term for the mother tree. "It [original sin] is the womb in which all actual sins are conceived," noted Thomas Watson (1620–86). "Hence come murders, adulteries, rapines. Though actual sins may be more scandalous, yet original sin is more heinous; the cause is more than the effect."[10]

The doctrine of original sin is humbling. Yes, I exaggerate, spend impulsively, speak unkindly, and fail to serve my spouse and children. But that is not the real issue. The problem is my nature, *who I am*, not what I do.

"Sins are nothing but the symptoms of a disease," noted D. Martyn Lloyd-Jones, himself a physician, "and it is not the symptoms that matter but the disease, for it is not the symptoms that kill but the disease."[11]

It would be a waste of money to see a doctor who treated strep throat with a topical salve rather than amoxicillin. In the same way, lying, stealing, selfishness, self-pity, lust, and complaining are symptoms. But the disease is sin, a fallen nature, the mother tree producing her saplings of pride and selfishness.

At the beginning of this chapter I noted that our culture is especially impervious to the doctrine of sin. An additional proof is that the majority of American Christians do not believe in original sin. "In a George Barna poll," writes R. C. Sproul, "more than seventy percent of 'professing evangelical Christians' in America expressed the belief that man is basically good. And more than eighty percent articulated the view that God helps those who help themselves."[12] In other words, the average evangelical believes that God relates to us on the basis of merit. This points to a radical breakdown in the gospel. The doctrine of original sin and the gospel are irrevocably connected. "Tell me what you think of sin," wrote Dr. William Plumer in the nineteenth century, "and I will tell you what you think of God, of Christ, of the Spirit, of the divine law, of the blessed Gospel, and of all necessary truth. . . . He, who sees no sin in himself, will feel no need of a Saviour. He who is conscious of no evil at work in his heart will desire no change of nature."[13]

Brothers and sisters, preach the doctrine of sin, share this doctrine with unbelievers, and counsel this doctrine with the troubled. You will do a great service to those you love.

When people see the truth about their fallen nature, all self-righteousness vanishes. They feel their desperate need for a Savior and for his salvation. "It's not what I do: It is who I am, and I can do nothing to change my nature. I'm in trouble. God, have mercy!" This is the heart cry of those who understand the holiness of God, their sinful nature, and the evil deeds it produces.

APPLICATION

The knowledge of sin is the door that we must walk through to find real happiness. There is an old saying: "To the degree that sin becomes bitter, grace becomes sweet." God equips us to exult in his grace, mercy, and love to the degree that the gospel strips us of our self-righteousness and deeply humbles us.

My family's water comes from a well. We always took fresh water for granted. Then one day our well pump went down. For two weeks we were without water. No hot showers. No tap water to drink. No dishwasher. We couldn't flush our toilets or wash clothes. By the time we finally fixed the pump, my perspective on water had changed. I had always taken flushing the toilet for granted, but now I thanked God for every flush. Before, I had taken running water for granted. Now I fixated on it, rejoiced in it, and was very appreciative of it. I wanted to "kiss the spout where the water comes out."

The knowledge of sin affects us the same way. Those who assume their own righteousness will take Christ, his cross, his grace, and his love for granted. They will be apathetic and lukewarm. But those who internalize the wrath of God (chapter 3), the final judgment (chapter 4), and their personal sinfulness (this chapter) will be red-hot with zeal. They will not be lukewarm. These truths make grace sweet. God's love becomes a Mount Everest, his mercies beyond description. Before, you took God's love and grace for granted. Now you know you are in deep trouble. You are not good. You deserve

119

judgment, and your best effort cannot change it. You are in great need, and the gospel is good news indeed.

God reveals himself to the humble, and the doctrine of sin is profoundly humbling. It weakens the power of original sin. It promotes the fear of God. All of God's blessings follow this humbling: "The fear of the LORD is the beginning of knowledge" (Prov. 1:7); "God . . . gives grace to the humble" (James 4:6). How does he grace them? He lets the humble see themselves in his light. God exalts the humble (Matt. 23:12). He exalts the humble with the knowledge of himself. "In every period where gospel faith has been strong and vigorous," notes Iain Murray, "the necessity of conviction of sin has been unquestioned by evangelical leaders."[14]

SUMMARY

The knowledge of sin is most humbling, but it is the door to the knowledge of God. If that is true, then helping others grow in humility should be the chief end of Christian ministry. This means that our evangelism, preaching, Bible studies, and counseling should all have this objective. This takes courage. The proud will resist humbling.

Christian counseling should start with the subject of sin and grace. When counseling, I never assume the gospel. Whether premarital counseling or working with the depressed, I always start with key diagnostic questions: "If an unbelieving friend asked you to describe the gospel, what would you say?" "If you were to die and come before Christ and he were to say, 'Why should I let you into heaven,' what would you say?" I am looking for them to articulate a clear grasp of their bankruptcy and God's infinite grace. I regularly get garbled, confusing answers—even from those who have attended my church for years.

Not just our counseling and witnessing, but also our preaching should be informed by the humbling content of Romans 1,

2, and 3. Good pastors preach expositorially through books of the Bible, but they should never do this to the exclusion of periodic sermons about the cross, sin, and our redemption.

Some subjects carry much more weight than the frequency of their appearance in the Bible seems to indicate. We need to return to them on a regular basis. The doctrine of God's wrath, the judgment to come, and our personal sin are a few of those subjects. Another is the subject of the next chapter, justification by faith alone.

6

Humbled by Faith Alone

Justification by faith alone is *articulus stantis vel cadentis ecclesia*—the article of faith which decides whether the church is standing or falling. . . . [It] is like Atlas: it bears a world on its shoulders, the entire evangelical knowledge of saving grace. . . . When Atlas falls, everything that rested on his shoulders comes crashing down too.

—J. I. Packer[1]

WHAT IS MORE HUMBLING than bankruptcy? A person finds himself unable to pay his debts. Expenses exceed income. He is in utter want. His assets no longer belong to him.

That was the experience of the Christian author J. C. Ryle (1816–1900). John Charles Ryle was born into a family of immense wealth and social status. Think Mr. Darcy in *Pride and Prejudice*. J. C. was the oldest son, and he lacked no comfort. In England, the oldest son of a wealthy family was expected to seek a career in Parliament, and that was Ryle's ambition.

He attended Eton. Then in 1834 he entered Christ Church, Oxford. He was an excellent student, earning scholarships and competing favorably with his academic peers. Tall, broad-shouldered, and handsome, he excelled at rowing and cricket. Of this manliness others would later write, "His virile personality dominated two generations of Evangelicals, and set an ineradicable mark upon a third."[2]

At age twenty-one, he suffered a protracted lung infection. During his confinement, he began to read the Bible, something that, according to his own admission, he had not done for fourteen years. A few weeks later, he entered an Oxford church just as Ephesians 2:8 was being read: "For by grace you have been saved through faith. And this is not your own doing; it is the gift of God." Ryle came under great conviction. "From that moment to the last recorded syllable of his life," notes one of his biographers, "no doubt ever lingered in John's mind that the Word of God was living and powerful, sharper than any two-edged sword."[3]

After graduation, Ryle returned to live with his parents. He was a "gentleman," an English term for one who would never have to work. So he began to prepare for a life in politics.

One morning he awoke to the sudden and unexpected news that his father's bank, unable to pay its debts, had gone into receivership. Overnight the Ryle family lost Henbury, their magnificent estate, with all its attendant wealth. The event scarred Ryle for the rest of his life. Years later he wrote, "We got up one summer's morning with all the world before us as usual, and went to bed that same night completely and entirely ruined. The immediate consequences were bitter and painful in the extreme, and humiliating to the utmost degree."[4] Raised in opulence, he had not expected to work for a living. Now, like everyone else, Ryle needed a job. He entered the ministry. The rest is history.

Note the quote above. "The immediate consequences [of the bankruptcy] were . . . *humiliating to the utmost degree.*" Ryle was materially bankrupt. In the same way, the unconverted person is spiritually bankrupt. Like material bankruptcy, spiritual bankruptcy is extremely humbling, but it is necessary preparation for God's glorious gift of justification.

SPIRITUAL BANKRUPTCY

The previous three chapters have discussed Romans 1:18–3:20—the wrath of God, the day of judgment, and the utter sinfulness of all people. Paul has labored to convince his readers that they are spiritually bankrupt. But there is a profound difference between financial and spiritual bankruptcy. Those who are financially bankrupt usually know it. Yet one can be spiritually bankrupt and be completely unaware of his condition. The words of Jesus quoted by the apostle John (appearing in the previous chapter) describe this person: "For you say, I am rich, I have prospered, and I need nothing, not realizing that you are wretched, pitiable, poor, blind, and naked" (Rev. 3:17). A man with $100 million in the bank has no interest in $10,000. But to someone who is bankrupt, $1,000 is good news indeed. This is our problem. We think we are rich when in fact we are bankrupt. Therefore, God must open our eyes.

Bankrupt people must plead for mercy. But pride does not like to beg. We would rather be on the giving end. We would rather pay for a friend's meal than have him pay for us. We would rather give charity than take it. But the gospel says that you must stoop to enter God's kingdom. God will be no man's debtor. He needs nothing. He will do the giving, and in the process strip us of all grounds for boasting: "For by grace you have been saved through faith. And this is not your own doing; it is the gift of God, not a result of works, *so that no one may boast*" (Eph. 2:8–9). What surprises us is that the transfer of boasting from self to God brings rest, confidence, and peace.

An aging Catholic friend close to death believed he would go to purgatory to work off his sin. Purgatory is just an after-death expression of self-salvation. It is a form of self-atonement. To break out of this mind-set, my friend needed to see his bankruptcy. I began with a gentle description of the bad news. He became very agitated. "I don't like your Protestant God. He is too severe and angry."

"I don't understand," I responded. "You would rather work it off in the flames of purgatory for thousands of years than believe the good news. I am not sure you understand what I am telling you. Jesus already did the work. He took the suffering that you expect in purgatory. He did this because he loves you. If you trust in Christ's work on the cross, you will go straight to heaven."

In his case, none of my pleading was effective. He was not going to take a handout from God. He would not be indebted to God.

By contrast, those prepared by the bad news rejoice in the good news. At the end of Romans 3, Paul explains the good news with 129 pungent words:

> But now the *righteousness* of God has been manifested apart from the law, although the Law and the Prophets bear witness to it—the righteousness of God *through faith in Jesus Christ* for all who believe. For there is no distinction: for all have sinned and fall short of the glory of God, and are *justified by his grace as a gift*, through the redemption that is in Christ Jesus, whom God put forward as a propitiation by his blood, to be received by faith. This was to show God's righteousness, because in his divine forbearance he had passed over former sins. It was to show his righteousness at the present time, so that he might be just and the justifier of the one who has faith in Jesus. (Rom. 3:21–26)

Let's pause to think hard about these verses. Paul uses dense, compact language to describe God's solution to our problem. The solution is as humbling as the problem. Because we are bankrupt, unable to help ourselves, God did it all. We are like a crippled man, unable to walk, moved from place to place by God.

This paragraph is the heart and soul of the gospel. According to Martin Luther, it is possibly the most important paragraph in the Bible.[5] Professor C. E. B. Cranfield calls it "the centre and heart" of the whole main section of Paul's letter to the Romans. Dr. Leon Morris suggests that it is "possibly the most important single paragraph ever written."[6] In this paragraph Paul tells us four things:

- First, he tells us *why* God acted.
- Second, Paul tells us *what* God did.
- Third, he tells us *how* God did this.
- And fourth, he tells us how to appropriate the benefit of Christ's work.

WHY HAS GOD ACTED?

First, Paul tells us why God has acted. Verse 23 sums up all that he previously said in Romans 1:18–3:20 with the phrase, "All have sinned and fall short of the glory of God." This means that everyone, Jew and Gentile, is under the all-pervading power of sin. It means that sin keeps us from glorifying God, which is the reason for our creation. Instead, we live for self. We live for private, narrow interests. We do not worship God or love him above all things. We worship everything but God. Most importantly, we worship self. God had to act because we are bankrupt.

In addition, he acted because "God is love" (1 John 4:16).

WHAT HAS GOD DONE?

Second, Paul tells us that God saves us by doing several things. First God justifies those who believe. *Justification* is a legal term. It is a declaration of righteousness. Justification occurs when the jury foreman rises and declares, "Not guilty." The opposite of justification is condemnation. Justification is the final verdict that the saints will receive on the day of judgment. It is the declaration of "not guilty" that we will carry into eternity, a declaration that can never be lost or tarnished.

Second, God justifies us on the basis of grace. We "are justified by his grace." Our salvation is a gift. God gives it to the guilty because they believe, not because they work. The technical definition of *grace* is "favor given to those who deserve punishment." If a judge were to award a defendant who murdered one of his children a million dollars and a free pass from jail, that would be grace—favor given to one who deserves punishment.

In other words, here is the good news. God saves those who believe. This gift cannot be earned. If it could, justification would be merited and would not be grace. But biblical justification is always a gift of sovereign grace.

HOW HAS GOD SAVED US?

Third, this passage tells us that God saves us by doing two things. First he has propitiated his own wrath with the blood of his Son. Second, and even more amazingly, he has done this without compromising his righteousness.

God propitiated his wrath with his Son's blood. The first half of Romans 3:25 might be the most important verse in the Bible: "God put forward [Christ Jesus] as a propitiation by his blood, to be received by faith." God solved the wrath problem, described by Paul in Romans 1:18–32, and he did it in a way that establishes and upholds his righteousness. He sent his Son to "propitiate" himself. *Propitiation* is an old word little used in modern vocabulary, so an explanation is in order.

We propitiate someone when we do something to pacify that person's anger, when we do something to restore a broken relationship, when we do something to make peace where anger once reigned. A husband staggers home drunk after a night out with the boys. His wife is furious. The next morning he takes her out to breakfast and presents her with a bottle of expensive perfume. He is propitiating her. He is doing something to remove her anger.

A daughter wrecks the family car. She has no collision insurance. She pleads with her father for mercy and promises to give him all her earnings until the debt is erased. What is she doing? She is propitiating her father's anger.

One reason "propitiation" is sometimes absent from translations of Romans 3:25 is that the word implies anger. The concept of propitiation suggests that, because of sin, the basic relationship between God and man is hostility. Naturally, as we saw in chapter 3, none of us want to think of God this way. We want to think of him as the great Panda Bear in the sky, approving of all, and dispensing good things to everyone.

We have a predicament. A husband can propitiate his wife, a daughter can propitiate her father, but there is nothing I can give God that will propitiate him. I have offended him too deeply. We are helpless. Human effort cannot solve this problem. Therefore, God must do the propitiating. God himself must provide the necessary blood sacrifice.

That brings up the messy subject of blood. Why blood? Because only faith in Christ's shed blood can propitiate God. "God put forward [Christ Jesus] as a propitiation by his blood." Why not propitiation by vegetable offerings, grain offerings, human sacrifice, death, purgatory, or even money? Why does propitiation require blood?

The answer begins with the idea that the penalty for sin is, and always has been, death. God told Adam, "In the day that you eat of it you shall surely die" (Gen. 2:17). And Paul adds,

"The wages of sin is death" (Rom. 6:23). The death threatened was both spiritual and physical.

In addition, in ancient times blood was a sign of life. The patriarchs noticed that when sufficient blood left the body, death followed. In other words, the shedding of blood signified death. From this the ancients developed the saying "the life of the victim is in its blood." Leviticus 17:11 is an example of this concept: "For the life of the flesh is in the blood, and I have given it for you on the altar to make atonement for your souls, for it is the blood that makes atonement by the life."

For this reason Christ's blood matters. It signifies death. It points to the satisfaction of God's justice. It says that the punishment for sin—death—has been meted out. The penalty for sin has been paid. Jesus paid it in our place. He died as our substitute.

If God, in the form of his Son, shed his own blood to propitiate himself, you can be confident that the war is over. God's wrath has been propitiated. Why? There is a profound and right correlation between the seriousness of your sin and the dignity of the sacrifice. Christ's blood balanced the scales of justice. The one who was angry, God, took the initiative to propitiate his own anger.

The cross is the measure of God's love. Because Jesus was infinite in dignity and value, the expense to God was infinite. What motivated him? Love! Extravagant love. Holy love. Infinite love! This is the context of John 3:16, "God so loved the world, that he gave his only Son."

Second, not only did God propitiate his wrath with his Son's shed blood, but he also did this without compromising his righteousness. Rather, he saved us by glorifying the beauty of his righteousness. This is the thrust of the last half of Romans 3:25 and verse 26: "This [the cross] was to show God's righteousness, because in his divine forbearance he had passed over former sins. It was to show his righteousness at the present time, so that he might be just and the justifier of the one who has faith in Jesus."

Righteousness is a term for the cumulative basket of God's moral perfections. God's love is one attribute in the basket. God is love (1 John 4:16). His heart yearned to save a sinful, fallen people. But God's justice is also in the basket: "Righteousness and justice are the foundation of [his] throne" (Ps. 89:14). Justice demands satisfaction. As the perfectly just Judge, God must punish sin. God's righteousness demanded that he save in a way that established, rather than compromised, his justice. Sin had to be punished before it could be forgiven. This presented a huge puzzle that only God's wisdom could solve.

Here is how God solved it. He sent his Son to be our substitute. He put our sins on Jesus' shoulders, and then sent him to the cross to receive the justice we deserve. As Jesus expired, God was both satisfying justice by punishing sin and also forgiving sinners. The cross simultaneously satisfied the yearnings of God's justice and the greatness of his love. It displayed both the beauty of his wrath and the perfections of his justice. The cross did this while manifesting the greatest display of grace in human history. The net effect was the salvation of needy sinners by vindicating both God's love and his justice.

This is why Paul referenced God's *divine forbearance when he had passed over former sins.* The cross convinces us that God never "winks at sin." It says, "I never take sin lightly. Rather, I always punish it." The Old Testament saints probably thought God forgave David's adultery and murder without satisfying justice. Romans 3:25–26 convinces us that this was not the case. God was able to pass over former sins, and he was able to forgive the sins of Abraham, Samson, and David, because he would later punish them in the death of Christ. At the cross,

131

the sins of the Old Testament saints, like ours, were punished so that God could then forgive.

HOW SHOULD WE RESPOND?

Fourth, Paul tells us how to respond. It is not enough to believe that all this happened. We must respond appropriately.

The sure way to forfeit the benefits of Christ's atonement is to deliberately work for them. Those who "work" do so because they reject their sinfulness and the need for the Father's gift, his Son. God takes it personally. When we respond to the gospel by working, the bad news has not done its job. The listener has not been humbled. The potential convert still retains a flicker of hope in his own goodness. God is not *that* holy (i.e., he is not angry; his standards are not that high; we are not *that* sinful. We can propitiate God by trying harder).

This is why there was a Reformation. It was not a squabble over secondary details. It was a battle for the souls of men. Heaven and hell hung in the balance. "Because imputed righteousness is directly contrary to human pride and self-sufficiency," notes Iain Murray, "it has always been opposed by a world hostile to Christ."[7]

The Roman church refused to confess this bankruptcy. Rome sought salvation through human merit. To the Reformers, this was a rejection of the gospel, and although the Catholics believed that Jesus died for their sins, Martin Luther and John Calvin knew that the rejection of justification by faith alone was no small issue.[8] The church rejected the cross of Christ. If I can earn salvation, Jesus did not need to die. If this is true, then confidence in our virtues sends more people to hell than all our other sins combined.

We appropriate the benefits of the good news only by renouncing our virtues and works, confessing our bankruptcy, and transferring trust from our works to Christ's alone.

Salvation is a gift. It cannot be earned. Christ saves those willing to admit their bankruptcy, humble themselves, and live by faith in God's grace.

APPLICATION

When we counsel struggling friends, we must remember that failure to believe in justification by faith alone is often their problem. They feel guilty, depressed, or discouraged precisely because they have reverted to measuring their relationship with God by their performance. It is our job to gently resketch the grace of God so that they can walk in the glorious freedom that is theirs in Christ. This is why James Buchanan, a nineteenth-century Scottish theologian, wrote:

> The best preparation for the study of justification is neither great intellectual ability, nor much scholastic learning—but a conscience impressed with a sense of our actual condition before God. A deep conviction of sin is the one thing needful in such an inquiry,—a conviction of the fact of sin, as an awful reality in our own personal experience,—as an inveterate evil cleaving to us continually, and having its roots deep in the innermost recesses of our hearts . . . which has deserved His wrath and righteous condemnation.[9]

The same is true when conducting personal evangelism. Unwillingness to accept justification by faith alone is often the problem. People do not see their need. It is our job to convince them of their great need. Once God opens people's eyes to their bankruptcy, conversions usually follow. In addition, conversions that begin with a thorough grounding in our personal bankruptcy have great staying power. They produce long-term fruit. Don't take shortcuts. Don't bypass your friends' immense need. Give them good reading materials. Take your time. Let the Word of God do its work in them.

Justification by faith alone is often our congregation's greatest need. It is easy for them to lose sight of the grace of God, to revert to earning God's favor. This should not surprise us. Justification by faith alone is a fragile flower. The leader convinced of this truth will repeatedly return to the theme of human bankruptcy and God's immense grace and goodness. He never presumes that his congregation is living in the daily joy of God's infinitely wonderful grace. He presumes just the opposite.

SUMMARY

We have come full circle. Chapters 1 and 2 suggested that efficacious saving faith humbles those who possess it. Chapter 3–6 examined Paul's preaching of his gospel. He began with bad news in order to humble sinners and motivate them to embrace God's gift of salvation.

J. C. Ryle became financially bankrupt, but we are spiritually bankrupt. The gospel is sweet to all who confess their need. It humbles us. It makes us beggars for mercy, but we beg from One who is an infinitely gracious Giver.

The gospel motivates us to transfer our trust from our works to Christ's. Those who do discover the love of God that surpasses knowledge.

By this we know love, that he laid down his life for us. (1 John 3:16)

In this is love, not that we have loved God but that he loved us and sent his Son to be the propitiation for our sins. (1 John 4:10)

7

Humbled by the History of Preaching

In every period where gospel faith has been strong and vigorous, the necessity of conviction of sin has been unquestioned by evangelical leaders.

—Iain Murray[1]

THIS CHAPTER WILL EXAMINE our thesis in light of church history. Has Paul's method of gospel preaching worked in the real world since the Reformation? A quick survey of church experience since the Reformation confirms one thing: the power of the gospel rides in a chariot that humbles sinners.

Every revival of lasting significance has produced conscience-searing convictions of sin. They are the necessary precedent for God's extravagant grace. God owns a gospel that humbles sinners. He owns it by sending spiritual power. As Brian Edwards notes in his book *Revival! A People Saturated with God*, "God prefers light to heat, and holiness to happiness."[2] Here is one eyewitness description of the 1907 revival that began the modern transformation of Korea:

As the prayer continued, a spirit of heaviness and sorrow for sin came down upon the audience. Over on one side, someone began to weep, and in a moment the whole audience was weeping. Man after man would rise, confess his sins, break down and weep, and then throw himself to the floor and beat the floor with his fists in perfect agony of conviction. My own cook tried to make a confession, broke down in the midst of it, and cried to me across the room: "Pastor, tell me, is there any hope for me, can I be forgiven?" and then he threw himself to the floor and wept and wept, and almost screamed in agony.[3]

The length, depth, and penetration of the gospel depend on the length and depth of our conviction about sin. This is a fundamental lesson from church history. The doctrines of sin, final judgment, the wrath of God, and justification by faith alone are crucial to this work. They are gospel basics, and they matter. Dr. Albert Mohler notes, "Preaching is deadly business. As Spurgeon confirmed, 'Life, death, hell, and worlds unknown may hang on the preaching and hearing of a sermon.' "[4] This lesson applies to any communication of the gospel, whether witnessing to a friend or counseling a Christian brother.

The church should never presume the gospel. Just the opposite. We should presume the fragility of the gospel. It is a delicate flower, easily wilted by religious pride, one that flourishes only when careful attempts to humble the church have been consistently applied. According to the great Scottish divine James Buchanan (1804–70), Martin Luther "knew that men would invariably grow indifferent to [justification by faith alone], in proportion as they became less impressed with *a sense of sin,* and less alive to *the claims of the Law* and *Justice of God.*"[5] The gospel is a shy bird. It flits away wherever and whenever the bad news is not emphasized.

For this reason, the Reformers (and all who have followed them) have felt the power of God, and his manifest presence, to the degree that they have emphasized the profound problem that men face and that Paul describes in Romans 1:18–3:20. This chapter will survey some of the high points of church history since the Reformation to make that point. In each case, spiritual revival and vitality have followed the persistent proclamation of "Christ and him crucified." This is the gospel message that humbles sinners.

THE REFORMATION

Oxford theologian Alister McGrath observes that

> by late 1514 Luther (1483–1546) had arrived at the fundamental insight that the proper disposition for justification is *humility*. . . . *God humiliates man, in order that he may justify him*; he makes man a sinner, in order that he may make him righteous—and both aspects of this matter are increasingly seen by Luther as works *of God.*[6]

After careful study of Paul, Luther saw that the goal of the gospel was a humbling faith.

In the autumn of 1517, Luther inadvertently initiated the Reformation by quietly posting his Ninety-five Theses on the Wittenberg church door. As we have seen, Luther was absolutely convinced of humanity's blindness to the truth about itself, and Luther knew that pride was the culprit. Luther, more than any other Reformer, saw the bad news with clarity. His biographer, Roland Bainton, quotes these words: "God hides his power in weakness, his wisdom in folly, his goodness in severity, his justice in sins, his mercy in his wrath."[7] To get to God's power, you must first become weak. To become wise, you must become foolish. To find and experience God's goodness, you must first face up to his severity as it appears in the doctrines of hell and final judgment. To understand

God's justice, you must first come face-to-face with your sin. And to experience his mercy, you must familiarize yourself with his wrath.

The perspective of the twenty-first-century church is generally the opposite. We want to know the mercy, grace, and love of God without going through God's wrath, his judgments, or our utter sinfulness. Thus, we are unlikely to find what we are looking for.

Summing up Luther's thinking, Bainton wrote:

> God works by contraries so that a man feels himself to be lost in the very moment when he is on the point of being saved. When God is about to justify a man, he damns him. Whom he would make alive he must first kill. God's favor is so communicated in the form of wrath that it seems farthest when it is at hand. . . . When he believes himself to be utterly lost, light breaks. Peace comes in the word of Christ through faith.[8]

Luther thought that a man will not run to Christ for justification until he feels the weight of damnation. The conviction that I am under God's wrath is a first sign of his favor toward me. Not until I have been profoundly humbled will the peace of Christ answer my need.

All of this Luther summed up in his most important theological work, *The Bondage of the Will. Bondage* was Luther's response to a work by Desiderius Erasmus (1456–1536), *A Diatribe Concerning the Freedom of the Will*[9] (1524). Erasmus was the greatest intellect of his day. He was a cynical Roman Catholic thought to be sympathetic with Luther. He was under great pressure to take a stand. Was he for or against the disruptive Reformer? His *Diatribe* was an attempt to stake out his position.

The doctrine Erasmus chose to debate is not one we would pick. He didn't start with the obvious—the authority of Scripture, or justification by faith alone. He tackled the bondage of the will. When theologians talk about the bondage of the will, they are not saying that I am not free to marry whom I like, or take a job in a neighboring state. The bondage of the will is about the effect of sin on my willingness and ability to choose to follow God.

Erasmus saw that the bondage or freedom of the will was the practical question on which the Reformation turned. How serious is sin? How great is its impact? Has the fall so crippled my will that I am unable to seek God, desire God, or turn to God without divine aid? Or will men and women seek and find salvation for themselves?

In effect, Erasmus said, "Sin is not prohibitively serious: The will is free." In *The Bondage of the Will* Luther responded that sin runs deep: the will is bound! In his conclusion, Luther made this important observation to Erasmus:

> I give you hearty praise and commendation on this fur-
> ther account—that you alone, in contrast with all others,
> have attacked the real thing, that is, the essential issue. You
> have not wearied me with those extraneous issues about
> the Papacy, purgatory, indulgences and such like—trifles,
> rather than issues—in respect of which almost all to date
> have sought my blood (though without success); you, and
> you alone, have seen the hinge on which all turns, and *aimed
> for the vital spot.*[10]

Purgatory and indulgences, "extraneous issues"? How could Luther say that? Because Luther knew that if sin bound the human will so that it could not and would not turn to God, then God must initiate my salvation. And unless salvation is by grace alone through faith alone, there is absolutely no hope. If salvation is by grace through faith alone, then the whole edifice of Roman Catholicism, built on works-righteousness, must come crashing down. The contended doctrines—purgatory, justification by works, the sacramental system, indulgences, the authority of the pope, the need for priestly mediation, and so forth—were just sophisticated ways of earning God's favor.

Luther and Erasmus agreed that the freedom of the will was the central issue. And human freedom was great or non-existent, depending on one's view of sin. Luther, not Erasmus, saw that unless the Reformation was a revival of the bad news, the gospel of the glorious grace and love of God would also be meaningless.

Like so many today, Erasmus felt that doctrine was unimportant, and the bondage of the will a superfluous issue. By contrast, Luther thought doctrine crucial, the bondage of the will important, and justification by faith alone "the very heart of the gospel."[11] Here is how Bainton described Luther's thought:

> Man's part, therefore, is to humble his proud mind, to renounce the sinful self-sufficiency which prompts him to treat himself as the measure of all things, to confess the blindness of his corrupt heart, and thankfully to receive the enlightening Word of God.[12]

This was not just Luther's view. The other Reformers stood in solidarity with Luther. "In asserting the helplessness of man in sin, and the sovereignty of God in grace, they [the magisterial Reformers] were entirely at one."[13] For example, in his *Institutes*, John Calvin (1509–64) wrote:

> I have always been exceedingly delighted with the words of Chrysostom, "The foundation of our philosophy is humility;" and still more with those of Augustine, "As the orator, when asked, What is the first precept in eloquence? answered, Delivery: What is the second? Delivery: What the third? Delivery:" so, if you ask me in regard to the precepts of the Christian Religion, I will answer, first, second, and third, Humility.[14]

Why is this important? On the surface the Reformation was about the authority of Scripture and justification by faith alone. Underneath, however, were stronger currents dealing with sin, man, and ultimate issues. The strength of the Reformation was its willingness to grapple with, and own, the wrath of God, the reality of final judgment, and the helplessness of man in sin. If these doctrines are true, and they are, there is no remedy but the grace proclaimed by Paul—justification by faith alone. This was the gospel the Reformers preached, and it turned the world upside down.

THE PURITAN ERA

Skip forward several decades to the high water of the Reformation, the Puritan era, approximately 1580 to 1680. Seventeenth-century England had about ten thousand parish pastors. Only about two thousand were Puritans, but their influence was completely out of proportion to their numbers. The preaching of these men helped to set the course of England for the next three centuries. Many scholars feel that Puritanism was a fundamental impetus for the rise of the British Empire, the development of capitalism, the emergence of modern science, and the spread of contemporary political freedom. Whether this was the case or not, we want to find the Puritans' secret and apply it.

First, the Puritans were ardent followers of the Reformation theology espoused by Luther and Calvin. Summing up their doctrine of justification, J. I. Packer writes that it was a matter "of divine revelation by grace. As such it is doubly *humbling*. It *humbles pride of intellect*, because it could never have been guessed or worked out by unaided religious reason, and it *humbles moral pride* by assuming that all men are hopeless and helpless in sin." The Puritans believed that "the mystery of justification is thus threatened constantly by *human pride*."[15]

Like Luther, the Puritans were convinced that the gospel is a fragile flower, one that will wither without constant attention. The bad news is the fertilizer that makes that flower healthy and strong.

Second, they were committed to preaching. For them this was primary. Their methods were diverse, but the message always came back to the gospel. They began with man's predicament in sin. J. I. Packer continues, "They diagnosed *the plight of man* as one, not merely of guilt for sins, but also of pollution in sin and bondage to sin. And by bondage to sin they meant; not bondage to *sins*—particular weaknesses of character and bad habits—but the state of being wholly dominated by an inbred attitude of habits of enmity to God." Packer states further, "They sought to expose the sinfulness that underlies sins, and convince men of their own utter corruption and inability to improve themselves in God's sight. This, they held, *was a vital part of the work of a gospel preacher,* for the index of the soundness of a man's faith in Christ is the genuineness of the *self-despair from which it springs.*"[16]

Third, the Puritans aimed their verbal arrows directly at their listener's conscience. In *Worldly Saints,* his insightful study of the Puritans, Leland Ryken writes, "It was said of Richard Mather that he aimed 'to shoot his arrows not over people's heads but into their hearts and consciences.' . . . Baxter wrote, 'If our words be not sharpened, and pierce not as nails, they will hardly be felt by stony hearts.'" Ryken concludes, "This imagery of active attack and physical contact with the recipient captures exactly the Puritan ideal of affective preaching."[17] Here is how Jeremiah Burroughs (1599–1646), one of the great Puritan preachers, summed up the Puritan goal in preaching:

> If this [humility] is such a disposition that God so much looks at, it should teach the ministers of God who have to deal with God's Word. When they speak it, they must speak it in such a manner that it may gain fear and trembling, that the hearts

142

of people may be struck with fear and trembling. They must not come to dally and play with men's fancies, nor with their own wit; but when they come to speak the Word of God, in God's name, they should labor to speak it so that the hearts of their listeners may be struck with fear and trembling.[18]

Sadly, toward the end of the Puritan era, 1675–1700, all of this began to unravel and decline. The church began to assume sin, the final judgment, the wrath of God, and human moral bankruptcy. The gospel flower began to wither. The result was predictable. Human pride was left untouched, and proud believers grew apathetic. The church became cold, formal, outwardly religious, moralistic, and substantially compromised by the world.

THE GREAT AWAKENING

Into this icy climate God sent white-hot grace. The key leaders used by God were George Whitefield (England, Wales, Ireland, Scotland, and North America), John Wesley (England), Jonathan Edwards (North America), and Daniel Rowland (Wales).

Although the awakening began in the mid-1730s, its high water was 1740–42. On both sides of the Atlantic godly men, energized by the power of the Holy Spirit, once again preached the utter bankruptcy of man and the free grace of God. It was a revival of massive proportions, maybe the greatest the world has seen. Twenty-four-year-old George Whitefield preached two-hour sermons to open-air London crowds estimated at twenty-five thousand to fifty thousand. When he came to Boston, the city's population was only ten thousand, yet crowds of fifteen thousand came to hear. It is difficult to rightly understand the modern world without reference to this epic period.

The theology and preaching of the New England pastor Jonathan Edwards (1703–58) represents this group. He tilled stony hearts with the bad news in order to sow the gospel of God's grace. His ultimate goal was a great harvest. Like Luther, he assumed that pride was the problem, the great obstacle to conversion. His sermon "Sinners in the Hands of an Angry God" (probably preached multiple times during the summer of 1741) is a good example of his methods. His main points were "1.) There is no want of *power* in God to cast wicked men into hell at any moment. 2.) They *deserve* to be cast into hell. 3.) They are already under a sentence of condemnation to hell. 4.) They are now the objects of that very same *anger* and wrath of God, that is expressed in the torments of hell. 5.) The *devil* stands ready to fall upon them, and seize them as his own, at what moment God shall permit him."[19] We know the response to this sermon when he gave it at Enfield, Connecticut, in the summer of 1741. His listeners came under such conviction that their cries of agony drowned out Edwards's voice. He had to end the sermon prematurely.

The question is not whether these methods would work today. The issue is, "Were Edwards's facts true? Were his methods biblical? Will God work his power through messages like this today?" The answer is a resounding "Yes!" Neither people nor God's methods have changed.

My wife and I were honored to visit the Beinecke Rare Book and Manuscript Library at Yale University. Edwards's manuscripts are archived there. We enjoyed the immense privilege of holding the original scraps of paper on which Edwards had written "Sinners." His handwriting was minute, but the concepts were immense. The sermon had one goal—to humble human pride and exalt Christ, to strip the human heart of all proud pretensions, and to prepare it for the amazing grace latent in the gospel.

Edwards preached many similar sermons. The titles are instructive. "Natural Men in a Dreadful Condition," "God Makes Men Sensible of Their Misery before He Reveals His Mercy and Love," "Men Naturally God's Enemies," and "The Final Judgment" are all examples. His compatriots—Wesley, Whitefield, and Rowland—shared similar convictions and methods.

As with the Reformers and the Puritans, during the Great Awakening the Holy Spirit resurrected doctrines that had been presumed, rejected, or forgotten. Edwards's major theological works defended subjects such as *Original Sin,* the *Bondage of the Will,* and *A Dissertation on the End for Which God Created the World.* In one of his masterpieces, *Religious Affections,* Edwards put his finger on the central issue:

> [Humility] is a great and most essential thing in true religion. The whole frame of the gospel, and everything appertaining to the new covenant, and all God's dispensations towards fallen man, are calculated to bring to pass this effect in the hearts of men. They that are destitute of this, have no true religion, whatever profession they may make, and how high soever their religious affections may be.[20]

Edwards's younger friend George Whitefield (1714–70), considered by many to be one of the most gifted preachers in history, followed a similar track. To do so, he had to conquer the fear of man. He put his mind on eternal things. "Before [his] mind he held a vision of the day when he would appear before the judgment seat of Christ," wrote his biographer, "and in the light of that accounting in eternity the affairs of time lost their importance. He was enabled to turn a deaf ear to the voices of men—whether in praise or blame—and sought only that his life should be worthy of the divine approval in that solemn hour. And this awareness of living beneath the all-searching eye of Omnipotence and of giving account remained a great underlying principle of his life."[21]

THE SECOND GREAT AWAKENING

By the 1750s, the Great Awakening had lost its momentum. Once again the church began to presume or reject the doctrines of sin, the final judgment, and the wrath of God. With their fading, the doctrines of justification by faith alone and the free grace of God also became scarce. They became memories of a bygone age. Into this vacuum God's Spirit came in a Second Great Awakening (roughly 1790–1830). Many key leaders emerged on both sides of the Atlantic. Even though his was a household name in the early decades of the nineteenth century, few today have heard of Asahel Nettleton (1783–1844). He was a New England evangelist whose message paralleled that of Edwards, Luther, and the Puritans before him. He would receive an invitation to evangelize the church in a town, take up residence, and preach for a week or two. Nettleton always began with the bad news, slowly humbling the proud, seeking to motivate his hearers to flee to the gospel for salvation. Here is one eyewitness account:

This evening will never be forgotten. The scene is beyond description. Did you ever witness two hundred sinners, with one accord in one place, weeping for their sins? Until you have seen this, you have no adequate conception of the solemn scene. I felt as though I was standing on the verge of the eternal world; while the floor under my feet was shaken by the trembling of anxious souls in view of a judgment to come. The solemnity was still heightened, when every knee was bent at the throne of grace, and the intervening silence of the voice of prayer was interrupted only by the sighs and sobs of anxious souls. I have no time to relate interesting particulars. I only add that some of the most stout, hard-hearted, heaven-daring rebels have been in the most awful distress.[22]

At the same time, on the other side of the Atlantic, Charles Simeon (1759–1836), preaching at Holy Trinity Church, Cambridge, made a huge impact. According to his biographer, Handley Moule, "Simeon himself thus describes the three great aims of all his preaching: 'To *humble the sinner*, To exalt the Saviour, To promote holiness.' Such was the heart and soul of his message. Whatever else he taught, all was gathered round these two foci, the sin of man and the glory of the Redeemer."[23]

Oh, brothers and sisters, how far has the modern church strayed from these aims. The words of Reinhold Niebuhr describe many of our churches: "A God without wrath brought men without sin into a kingdom without judgment by the ministration of a Christ without a cross." Thankfully, many of us would respond, "This does not describe me or my church." But unless we pay careful and repeated attention to the bad news, his words will describe the next generation.

One of my favorite preachers of the Second Great Awakening was Edward Payson (1783–1827), who experienced a constant stream of conversions. His posthumous biography was one of the most popular of the nineteenth century. Do an Internet search for Edward Payson and note the hundreds of nineteenth-century children named after him.

In his early twenties, Payson began to see his sinfulness through God's eyes. A typical diary entry read, "Never appeared so exceedingly vile and loathsome to myself as I did this day. . . . I felt like sinking into the dust, in the idea that his pure eye was fixed upon me, and that saints and angels saw how vile I was."[24]

In 1807, at the age of twenty-four, he became pastor of the Congregational church in Portland, Maine. He preached there until his death in 1827. Such was the grace and power that attended his preaching that three churches in the area asked Payson to become their pastor. One even offered to build a new church for the multitudes that waited to hear him. A typical entry in Payson's diary at this time read, "Was not much assisted myself, but what was said seemed to come with power. Many were in tears, and all seemed stirred up; so that, though I went crushed down under discouragement, I came back rejoicing."[25]

Payson was an effective soul-winner. He did not build his congregation on disgruntled Christians from other churches. In addition, he did not number conversions spuriously. He did not consider one converted on the basis of the person's testimony alone. Rather, Payson, like the other pastors of his generation, waited until the new convert began to show signs of spiritual fruit. Only then did they consider the person converted.

With these limitations in mind, in September 1809 he wrote to his mother, "Last communion, we admitted eleven to the church, and next Sabbath we shall admit twelve more." He went on, "The appetite for hearing seems insatiable, and our assemblies are more crowded than ever. Many have lately joined us."[26] These comments typified Payson's experience. During the twenty years of his ministry, his church received more than seven hundred new converts.

What was the content of Payson's preaching? His sermons contained repeated references to the final judgment. "The fire of his anger must burn forever. It is a fire, which cannot be quenched, unless God should change or cease to exist. It is this, which constitutes the most terrible ingredient of that cup, which impenitent sinners must drink."[27] He repeatedly warned his listeners about hell: "Since your peace must be finally disturbed [in hell], is it not better, that it should be disturbed now, when true peace with God may be obtained, rather than hereafter, when it will avail nothing?"[28] The titles of his sermons are like those of Edwards:

"Sins Estimated by the Light of Heaven," "Our Sins Infinite in Number and Enormity," and "The Difficulty of Escaping the Damnation of Hell." The irony is that men such as Payson preached from deep wells of grace, compassion, and love. So other sermon titles were "Demonstration of Christ's Love" and "Christ's Special Tenderness towards Penitent Disciples."[29]

In addition, this kind of preaching motivated an unusually robust missionary movement. Compassionate, tender-hearted men and women went forth preaching this gospel. Why? They felt the wrath of God, the reality of the final judgment, and the utter sinfulness of man. Compassion and love for the lost compelled them. It started as a trickle but grew into the greatest missionary movement in history. Men such as John Paton (1824–1907) went to the South Pacific to evangelize the New Hebrides Islands. Adoniram Judson (1788–1850) left New England to evangelize the people of Burma. Hundreds joined William Carey (1764–1831) in India. Men such as Henry Martyn (1781–1812), influenced by Simeon, sailed from England to evangelize the peoples of India and Persia.

All of this was the fruit of preaching that sought to humble men and women. To the degree that this message disappears, the missionary impulse also declines and fades. In his book *The New Shape of World Christianity: How American Experience Affects Global Faith*,[30] Mark Noll, distinguished church historian, notes the devastating effect that theological liberalism has on missions. To the degree that any denomination comes under the influence of liberalism, the number of field missionaries reduces dramatically. Why evangelize if there is no wrath, no judgment, and no serious problem with sin? If people can merit heaven with good intentions, why is the gospel needed? These assumptions destroy the impulse for missions.

THE POWER OF A HUMBLING MINISTRY

The point of all this is that God empowers the person who preaches a humbling gospel. The preacher introduces others to what Jonathan Edwards called evangelical humiliation. It is "a sense that a Christian has of his own utter insufficiency, despicableness, and odiousness, with an answerable frame of heart."[31] God's power is most apt to visit this ministry. Why?

First, a humbling ministry grounds the listener in reality. We *should* feel exceedingly small and insignificant. When we compare our physical size with the universe, we are nothing, and God is *infinitely* larger than the universe. In addition, when compared with God's pristine, holy-white goodness, we are sinful, vile, dark, and repugnant. As we have already noted, the irony is that this insight makes one increasingly happy and holy.

Second, God empowers the ministry that communicates a humbling gospel because it works where God is working. God is always humbling sinners. In his book *A Praying Life*, Paul Miller writes, "If Satan's basic game plan is pride, seeking to draw us into his life of arrogance, then God's basic game plan is humility, drawing us into the life of his Son."[32] God's game plan is humility, and those who pursue it attract God's power.

Third, God empowers the humbling ministry because it is a God-glorifying ministry. God's glory is his ultimate purpose for creation and redemption. Humility is a by-product of seeing God in his glory. God glorified is also a by-product of a humbling gospel. The bigger God gets, the smaller we get in our own eyes. The more delightfully small we become, the more attractive God becomes. God empowers a humbling ministry because it is going where he is going.

Fourth, God empowers the humbling ministry because humility fortifies the saints for long-term fruitfulness. Humble saints persevere to the end. Twenty-nine years after the ministry of Asahel Nettleton, a pastor in one of the communities he evangelized, J. B. Clark, did a study of the long-term fruit of Nettleton's evangelism. Here are his conclusions: "Most of those who were connected with the church, as the result of that revival, have worn remarkably well, so far as is or can be known. Many of them have been, and are still, bright and shining lights in the church of Christ."[33]

Later, his biographer adds, "Given the extent of his exposure, and the permanence of his converts, he very well may have been, next to George Whitefield, the most effective evangelist in the history of the United States. . . . *Only a small fraction of his converts were spurious.*"[34] Very few evangelists can say that only a small fraction of their converts prove not to be genuine. What accounted for these results? Nettleton prepared his listeners for the good news with detailed attention to the bad news.

Fifth, as we noted in chapter 1, God empowers the ministry that preaches a humbling gospel because it is fruitful. Humility is the root system from which the other fruits sprout. "The fruit of the Spirit," notes Wayne Mack, is " 'love, joy, peace, patience, kindness, goodness, faithfulness, gentleness, self-control . . .' (Gal. 5:22–23). All of these godly traits are *manifestations of true humility.* Proud people lack love for others, joy in all situations, peace in their relationships with other people, and patience for difficulties. Only humble people consistently exhibit the characteristics listed in Galatians 5:22–23 because these traits are produced by the Holy Spirit in the life of the believer."[35]

If Mack's insights are true, and we want joyful, loving, enthusiastic disciples, then we need to consistently and repeatedly humble sinners in order to amplify their fruitfulness. This has been the lesson of church history.

SUMMARY

Throughout church history, whenever God has moved with power, his people have proclaimed the bad news in order to

151

prepare their hearers for the good news. In fact, this is one way to measure the intensity of God's presence. Do God's people feel the horror of sin? Do they understand what they deserve—crucifixion? Are the wrath of God and the justice of God real? Then, through the lens of these truths, have the love of God, the mercy of God, and the grace of God become infinitely precious and glorious?

This is the best way to measure God's presence. It is not "barking in the Spirit," "laughing in the Spirit," being "slain in the Spirit," or even mighty miracles. We want miracles, but they can occur without God's being present in a saving way (see Matt. 7:21–23). All of these the devil can counterfeit. But the things that neither the devil nor the flesh will ever attempt to counterfeit are genuine convictions of sin, the fear of God, and the subsequent peace with God that is a fruit of faith in the gospel. "Revival is always a revival of holiness," notes Brian Edwards. "And it begins with a terrible conviction of sin. It is often the form that this conviction of sin takes that trouble those who read of revival. Sometimes the experience is crushing. People weep uncontrollably, and worse! But there is no such thing as a revival without tears of conviction and sorrow."[36]

Could it be that the world does not take Christianity seriously because the church itself doesn't take it seriously? Is our main goal making people happy? Our job is not to make people happy but to make them holy. Is comforting people our primary end? Our primary job is not comforting the church. Our primary job is disturbing them in order to shake them from their lethargy. It is not our job to make religion fun. Our job is to make people feel their desperate need for Christ and his gospel, and that is often hard work. That has been the lesson of church history.

This was Paul's modus operandi:

And I, when I came to you, brothers, did not come proclaiming to you the testimony of God with lofty speech or wisdom. For I decided to know nothing among you except Jesus Christ and him crucified. And I was with you in weakness and in fear and much trembling, and my speech and my message were not in plausible words of wisdom, but in demonstration of the Spirit and of power, that your faith might not rest in the wisdom of men but in the power of God. (1 Cor. 2:1–5)

PART THREE

BECOMING A WORKER WHO HUMBLES!

Your minister may be an anointed bishop, he may be a gowned and hooded doctor, he may be a king's chaplain, he may be the minister of the largest and richest and the most learned parish in the city, but, unless he strikes terror and pain into your conscience every Sabbath, unless he makes you tremble every Sabbath under the eye and hand of God, he is no true minister to you. As Goodwin says, he is a wooden cannon.

—Alexander Whyte[1]

8

The Fear of Man
Is a Snare

"There is . . . no fear of God before their eyes." No fear
of God! There is fear of man; fear of losing his favor,
his love, his good-will, his help, his friendship; this is
seen everywhere. How do the poor fear the rich, the
weak fear the strong, and those that are threatened,
them that threaten? But come now to God. Why, none
fear him; that is, by nature, none reverence him; they
neither fear his frown, nor seek his favor, nor inquire
how they can escape his avenging hand that is lifted up
against their sins and their souls because of sin. Little
things, they fear the losing of them; but the soul they are
not afraid to lose! "They fear not me, saith the Lord."
—John Bunyan[1]

A GUEST PASTOR SPOKE on the love of God at a wed-
ding. I was there. He reminded the congregation that God
calls each husband to love his wife as Christ loved the church.

157

To unwrap this idea, he developed the concept of propitiation. Jesus did not die for his friends. He died for his enemies. He died to propitiate God's wrath, to make peace between God and man. In conclusion, he called on husbands to love their wives this same way. He also urged the unbelievers in attendance to admit their guilt, confess their sin, and believe that God had sent his Son to solve our wrath problem.

Like those who attend most weddings, this audience was composed of believers and unbelievers. Some responded with apathy. Others became angry. A few were mildly offended. But a few, like those who listened to Paul at the Areopagus, wanted to hear more. The speaker was a man of great courage. Obviously, the fear of man did not control him.

In the same way, our ability to help people grow in humility will be according to our ability to overcome the fear of man. We conquer the fear of man with the fear of God. The fear of God motivates us to seek his approval more than the applause of people. It frees us to trust in the sovereignty of God, not the influence of people.

We all experience the fear of man, some more than others. If you are unaware of it, pray that God will orchestrate the right circumstances to help you see it. A few months before I began to serve as a senior pastor at Grace Christian Fellowship, I attended a Christian leaders' conference. One of the breakout sessions was on the fear of man. "The fear of man is an important subject," I thought. "I am thankful that it doesn't apply to me." I didn't know myself. In the next twenty-four months, the fear of man began to ooze to the surface. There is nothing like the pressures of pastoral leadership to expose the fear of man.

North American pastors are not like those of Europe. We do not lead state-supported churches that are the only choice for those wishing to attend church. The state does not guarantee our salary.[2] Instead, we compete for members with other Christian churches, non-Christian religions, and the cultural fads of our day. Although church growth is not the sole measure of success, every pastor wants his church to grow. That includes me. Therefore, I experienced the temptation to please people by compromising the truth. In biblical language, I was tempted to fear man.

The most potent expression of fearing man is pragmatism. It occurs when the lust for church growth trumps the fear of God. It is the willingness to let "whatever works" determine our agenda. The bad news is usually the first casualty. As we have seen, it is inherently offensive. It splits lukewarm congregations. It provokes strong reactions. It often sparks contention. People respond either affirmatively or negatively, but there is little neutrality. But pragmatism did not control Paul. He was determined to grow the church God's way or not at all.

A pastor friend described his temptation to pragmatism. He preached the gospel beginning with the bad news. Like Paul, he spent a significant amount of his time there. Then, after the bad news had prepared his listeners, he joyfully explained the good news. But his church didn't grow. Instead, it began to shrink. Some longtime members complained. Visitors walked out in the middle of his sermons. New people visited, but only a few returned. He told me about a neighboring church that ignored the bad news and steadily grew. He began to question himself. *Maybe I am doing something wrong. Maybe my preaching is unbalanced. Have I become a fanatic? Have I gone too far?*

Relatives visited and complained. They associated the word *fundamentalist* with his name. *Maybe I should change the message*, he thought. *Maybe there is a kinder, gentler way to say it. Hell is a hard teaching. Informing them that they are sinners is probably a little over the top. Maybe I should wait until they are converted to discuss these things.* These temptations came, but by God's grace he persevered, convinced that the full counsel of God was powerful and efficacious. Slowly his church turned the corner and began to grow again. *Because* he conquered the fear of man, today he pastors a thriving congregation. The unity of his church is tighter, their fellowship deeper, and their relationships stronger. Why? His people have been humbled under the gospel. From that foundation the other virtues are now growing.

Paul faced a similar temptation. That is why he began his explanation of the gospel with these words: "I am not ashamed of the gospel" (Rom. 1:16). He inserted this verse here because he would need to overcome the fear of man to write the next three chapters of Romans. He knew these chapters would also tempt the church in Rome. In the same way, none of us are exempt from temptations to be ashamed of the gospel—to capitulate to the fear of man.

Because it disrupts gospel proclamation, overcoming the fear of man matters greatly. This is why Paul repeatedly exhorted Timothy: "Do not be *ashamed* of the testimony about our Lord, nor of me his prisoner, but share in suffering for the gospel by the power of God" (2 Tim. 1:8); "Do your best to present yourself to God as one approved, a worker who has no need to be *ashamed*, rightly handling the word of truth" (2:15). Paul knew this temptation personally. His proclamation of man's spiritual bankruptcy provoked much of his great persecution. No one gets persecuted for saying, "God loves you and has a wonderful plan for your life." This is why Paul reminded Timothy, "Indeed, all who desire to live a godly life in Christ Jesus will be persecuted" (3:12).

We can say with certainty that the fear of man (embarrassment or shame about the gospel) motivates most liberal theology. It motivates most sliding away from the truth. That is why orthodox Christians fight the fear of man. Don't be ashamed of the gospel. Embrace it! Boast in it! Identify with it! The foolishness of God is always wiser than the wisdom of man. What is cool seldom lasts. "If I am concerned as I preach this gospel as to what people think of my preaching," wrote

D. Martyn Lloyd-Jones, "well that is all that I will get out of it, and nothing from God. It is an absolute. If you are seeking a reward from men you will get it, but that is all you will get."[3]

SMALL CONGREGATIONS

Maybe you have preached the gospel, you have overcome the fear of man, but your congregation is small, and it is not growing. If you have made the bad news an end in itself, you should have a small congregation. We have all passed a street preacher thundering out judgment and wrath. In many of these cases the bad news has become an end in itself. It is not a bridge to the good news about God's mercy and grace. If this is you, and your congregation is small, I urge you to change. I urge you to use the bad news to preach the love of God and the hope implicit in the good news.

I want to address the person communicating the whole counsel of God, who uses the bad news to exalt the good news, but whose congregation is not growing. You should be encouraged. You are in good company. It took Noah approximately a hundred years to build the ark. During that time Peter reminds us that he heralded righteousness to his generation (2 Peter 2:5). He preached bad news followed by the good news of salvation: "A flood is coming. Believe; repent. Join me on the ark." He did this for a hundred years, all the while resisting the siren song of pragmatism. How many responded? When the flood came, only his wife, his sons, and their wives joined him. Noah, however, did not change his message to improve his results. "In reverent fear [he] constructed an ark" (Heb. 11:7). He feared God, not man. He remained faithful.

Think back on the prophets. None had large followings. None were popular. A minority followed Elijah, but the majority worshiped Baal. Those who worshiped Baal hated Elijah. The prophet became discouraged. "I, even I only, am left, and they seek my life, to take it away" (1 Kings 19:14). Everyone who faithfully preaches the bad news will at times feel like Elijah. How did God respond? "I will leave seven thousand in Israel, all the knees that have not bowed to Baal" (19:18). God was in control. The size of Elijah's following was not the issue. Faithfulness was the issue. Elijah feared God, and God used him to gather the elect. If we would be used by God, we also must conquer the fear of man.

Jeremiah is another example. Here is my summary of his message to Israel: "For centuries you have engaged in persistent idolatry. God is angry. The Babylonians are coming. God has summoned them. They are his servants. Submit to them. God has sent them to take you in chains to Babylon. That is your punishment. If you resist, your women will cannibalize their children. The Babylonians will destroy the temple, tear down Jerusalem's walls, burn what remains, and deport you in chains to a foreign land. After seventy years I will bring you back."

Are you surprised that Jeremiah had few if any followers? He was faithful, but it cost him. "My joy is gone; grief is upon me," he complained; "my heart is sick within me" (Jer. 8:18). It got so bad that he even mourned the day of his birth: "Woe is me, my mother, that you bore me, a man of strife and contention to the whole land! I have not lent, nor have I borrowed, yet all of them curse me" (15:10).

Note the crucial divide that separated the true from the false prophets. False prophets were light on sin. They did not seek to humble God's people. Instead, they "whitewashed" Israel's sin, minimizing its offense. "They have misled my people, saying, 'Peace,' when there is no peace," complained Ezekiel, and "when the people build a wall, these prophets smear it with whitewash" (Ezek. 13:10). The false prophets feared man, so they kept their message positive. Jeremiah protested, "They have spoken falsely of the LORD and have said, 'He will do nothing; no disaster will come upon us, nor shall we see sword or famine' " (Jer. 5:12). Here is how Micah described the message of the false prophets: "Disgrace will not overtake us" (Micah 2:6).

Jesus was the fulfillment of the Prophets, the consummation of all Old Testament oracles, and he referred to hell more often than anyone else in the Bible. He rebuked the Pharisees in the harshest language. He called them "a brood of snakes, false guides, fools." On them he pronounced seven woes. He warned them to flee from the wrath to come. He cautioned everyone who refused him that the wrath of God rested on them (John 3:36). He reminded Israel of the coming wrath (Luke 21:23). He was exceedingly clear about sin. His healings and exorcisms attracted thousands. He was like the prophets who preceded him. When all the dust had settled, there were only one hundred and twenty remaining in the upper room.

In summary, the false prophets emphasized the virtues of God's people, not their sins. Therefore, they had no place in their thinking for God's judgment. After all, they were good people. They were God's chosen people.

We have false prophets today, and their message is similar. They preach the good news without reference to the bad news. The gospel is the most positive message on the market, but faithful men access it through the bad news. The false prophets of old preached a positive message that had no room for bad news, and they were popular; so are the false prophets of today.

Important caveat: I am not saying that large churches are bad. In the nineteenth century, C. H. Spurgeon preached the bad news faithfully. His church was the largest in the English-speaking world.[4] In the twentieth century, D. Martyn Lloyd-Jones preached the bad news to thousands in downtown London.[5] John Piper faithfully ministers the truth to a large congregation in Minneapolis. Many other contemporary pastors preach the bad news to large and growing congregations.

For this I am deeply grateful. Rather, my point is this: on the day of judgment, God will hold us accountable not for the size of our congregations, but for our faithfulness to the message preached. Pursue faithfulness, not numbers. To do that, you must overcome the fear of man with the fear of God.

OVERCOMING THE FEAR OF MAN

You need to confront a key leader, but you fear his reaction. You fear a church split or the disapproval of those who admire him. You want to share the gospel with a parent, sibling, or work associate, but you fear their rejection. A friend comes to you for counsel. He is unable to forgive. He doesn't understand his sin, or what it cost Christ to forgive him. You need to tell him, but you are afraid. If you do, he may not return. A friend partakes of the Lord's Supper, but you know he is into sexual sin. You know you should confront him, but you are afraid of the fallout. Each circumstance mentioned is a gracious gift from God to help us identify and repent of the fear of man.

What causes the fear of man? There are two roots—unbelief and a failure of love. First, unbelief. We don't trust God to act. If I confront the leader in sexual sin, things might get ugly in the short run. If I ask my unbelieving relative about the gospel, she will mock me. No one has ever communicated the bad news to my congregation. If I start now, it will provoke dissension or complaints.

Faith in God's goodness (that is, his willingness to reward those who please him), belief in the power latent in the gospel, and confidence in God's sovereignty will cripple the fear of man. The fear of God begins with a robust faith in God's greatness and goodness. At one level the fear of God is a synonym for this kind of faith.

Iain Murray writes of the nineteenth-century Scottish missionaries, men who were especially good at fearing God. Of the preaching of men such as Robert Moffat (1795–1883), who evangelized the feared Zulu tribes of South Africa, he notes, "They kept back nothing of the seriousness of sin." Then he adds, "They defined [sin] in the light of the character of God." The Zulus were known for their brutality. Chaka, their former chief, was responsible for the slaughter of 2 million African natives. He routinely tortured those who aggravated him. Despite these facts, Moffat started with the bad news, and God gave him success. Why did Moffat do this? He knew that God's means get God's results. Eventually that is what happened. God sent his Holy Spirit to Moffat's ministry.[6]

Faith in God's greatness is the heart and soul of fearing God. We displace the fear of man with the fear of God. "If you are searching for one key principle to help you in your struggle with fear," writes Wayne Mack, "here it is. In order not to fear, you must begin to fear."[7] Mack means that we cure the fear of man with the fear of God. In the words of Ed Welch,[8] the fear of God makes God big and people small. This fear liberates us to preach the bad news, to confront Christians in unrepented sin, to speak the truth in counseling situations, and to tactfully include the bad news in our personal evangelism.

God is big enough to empower an honest, faithful explanation of the bad news in order to set up the good news. When there is fallout from this approach, which sometimes happens, those who fear God are confident that God will pick up the pieces. "All experiences of the fear of man share at least one common feature," notes Ed Welch. "People are big. They have grown to idolatrous proportions in our lives. They control us. Since there is no room in our hearts to worship both God and people, whenever people are big, God is not. Therefore, the first task in escaping the snare of the fear of man is to know that *God* is awesome and glorious, not other people."[9]

The faith at the heart of the fear of God also convinces us that the basic doctrines of the Christian faith are true. It convinces me that I will give an accounting to God on the day of judgment. I will not give an accounting to the people I currently fear. They do not control my life. God does, and he means me good, not harm. Spurgeon remarked, "Those eyes which have no fear of God before them now, shall have the terrors of hell before them forever."[10] In other words, fear God now or fear him later. Those are the only options, but fear him everyone will eventually do.

This kind of faith liberates us to please God and disappoint people. The greater our faith in God, the larger he looms, the more we fear him, and the less we fear people. By contrast, when we fear people, God becomes small and people become big. *What if they reject me? What if they slander or gossip about me? My life will be ruined. What if the boss fires me for sharing the gospel with a coworker?* The wrong response to these questions points to a small faith in a small God.

In addition to unbelief, there is a second reason we fear people. Our love is weak. It is impossible to fear the opinion of others and love them at the same time. The fear of man is need-centered: I need your love, your acceptance, your approval. But love, God's love, is always other-centered. God's love is your happiness at my expense. It is the willingness to be the cause of others' short-term pain for their eternal good.

The fear of man is a bondage, and love is the power that breaks its chains. It makes timid Christians bold, bashful Christians assertive, and complacent Christians involved.

It is important to know that the fear of God is not the absence of anxiety, stress, or worry. By contrast, the fear of God is the willingness to do the right thing for your brothers and sisters despite the fear of rejection, the fear of division, or the recognition that you are not perfect yourself. I have lain awake at night, stressed, because I knew I needed to confront someone at breakfast the following morning. Fearing God didn't make it easy, but it empowered me to do the right thing despite the stress and inner turmoil. In a fallen world, that is sometimes what love for God and man looks like.

Most importantly, be patient. Overcoming the fear of man is a lifelong process. Just when you think it's conquered, it will surface through a new set of circumstances. For most of us, the fear of man is a daily struggle. But the battle is worth the effort.

In summary, "the fear of man lays a snare" (Prov. 29:25). It is idolatry. Those who fear man bow down to the god of human approval. But there is good news. Jesus died to atone for this sin. Christ's cross is the measure of God's hatred for our idolatry. Seeing this motivates repentance. Christ's cross is also the measure of God's love for those "snared" by the fear of man. It gives us hope. When we capitulate to the fear of man, which we someday will, there is forgiveness. There is love from God. There is mercy. When Jesus said, "It is finished," the punishment for all our fear of man—past, present, and future—was over. God's wrath was exhausted. There is none left for those who believe the gospel.

PERSONAL EVANGELISM

How should we respond to this chapter? When appropriate, include the bad news in your efforts to evangelize. Use tracts that emphasize the bad news. *Are You Good Enough?* is one example. One of the men in our church just took an ex-Mormon through this pamphlet. When he came to the wrath of God, the unbeliever was visibly shaken. The humbling process had begun.

When appropriate, include the wrath of God in your witnessing. Always ask permission: "Do you mind if I tell you why the Bible calls the gospel *good news?*"

"No, I don't mind." "It is good news because it solves an important problem, one that each of us will someday face." Then gently explain sin, God's reaction (wrath), and the inevitability of judgment. This information is needed to prepare your listener for the good news. Until he or she is humbled, the gospel will be of little interest.

I recently had the opportunity to share the gospel with an old friend. Compared with most people, he is unusually moral. He is faithful to his wife, an excellent father, and an upright businessman. In fact, he takes great pride in his morality. That is why he is not a Christian. He feels no need for the gospel. One day he described some of the charitable boards on which he serves. I responded, "Compared to most people, you are very moral, but that will not help your relationship with God. In fact, your trust in your morality just makes your relationship with God worse."

Surprised, he said, "What do you mean?"

"God is holy. That means he is not like anything with which you or I are familiar. In his moral goodness he is utterly unlike us. His standard is beyond us. You must be perfect to get into heaven."

"No one is perfect," he responded with obvious concern.

Then he said, "I have many Christian friends. They have talked to me about Christianity. Why haven't they shared this with me?"

"I don't know," I responded.

I continued, "Because of your imperfections (what the Bible calls sin), God is angry with you. But God doesn't want to be angry. He wants reconciliation. He sent his Son to bear the anger that he feels for you. God poured out all the anger that he feels for you and your sins on Jesus Christ on the cross. He did this because he loves you and wants to be your friend. If you believe this, Jesus' death will reconcile you to God. But to get into heaven you must renounce your confidence in the good deeds that you just mentioned. They will not help you. Instead, you need to transfer your trust from them to Jesus Christ."

We talked for another fifteen minutes. In addition, we met for several weeks to discuss further. To my knowledge he has not yet become a Christian, but he has heard the gospel. I told him the truth because I believe with all my heart that the gospel is the power of God for salvation, and the gospel begins with bad news. I told him the truth to motivate him to humble himself in order to enter God's kingdom.

COUNSELING

Obviously, counseling is more involved than simply sharing the bad news or the good news. When appropriate, however, the bad news is useful in our counseling. For example, a Christian friend comes to you. He is struggling with his marriage. His mate's imperfections are consuming him. It is all he can talk about or think about. His problem is pride. He sees his mate's sin with 20/20 clarity, but he is blind to his own faults.

The cure is the humility that comes from a clear apprehension of his own sin, what he deserves, and what it cost God to forgive him. To help him, you must revisit the bad news. Christ died for him when he was God's enemy. He did this to secure God's forgiveness for sins infinitely serious in his sight. Yes, your spouse is a sinner, but you can't control your spouse. All you can control is your own behavior. Where have you sinned? Where have you failed?

Everything will change when your friend sees his own sin, what it cost Christ to forgive him, and how small his mate's sins are by comparison. The best way to achieve this is to revisit what your friend deserves, the wrath of God, the judgment from which Christ saved him, and his utter bankruptcy. Humble couples are happy couples. They are thankful. They focus on God's grace in their mates, not their sins.

If pride is the root of all evil, then it follows that pride must be behind most counseling problems. A clear presentation of the bad news is crucial to our humbling. Hearing the bad news once is not enough. We are leaky vessels. Most of us need repeated exposure to these truths.

PREACHING

The bad news is fundamental to all preaching and teaching. It must have a permanent home on our short list of important topics. We should always present the bad news to humble people, amplify the love of God, and deepen their dependence on God. "Sometimes the distinction is made in the popular mind between 'hellfire' preachers on the one hand and preachers that understand God's love on the other," writes Mark Dever. "But that distinction is no more than a caricature. The preacher who talks *only* about God's love talks about it less and less with every sermon they preach, because there is less in their own mind that God loves us in spite of."[11] Dever is right. To get to the love of God, we must discuss the bad news.

The most important form of pastoral preaching is expository. It persistently covers a book of the Bible from beginning to end. The gospel is the main story line of the Bible. Therefore, the preacher should routinely connect most texts to both the bad news and the good news inherent in the gospel. A healthy diet of sermons will also include occasional topical sermons on subjects such as the Trinity, the second coming, God's ultimate purpose, and the sacraments. They will also address the wrath of God, the sinfulness of man, and the judgment to come. They provide our congregations with a theological framework that elevates God and humbles man.

A friend's church shares the Lord's Supper on the first Sunday of every month. For the first five years that he was pastor, he took advantage of the Lord's Supper to preach a sermon on the atonement. The topics are endless. For example, he preached on God's use of the word *abomination* to describe

170

sin in the Old Testament and then showed how Christ went to the cross to become an abomination in our place.

He looked at the sin of "despising God" in the Old Testament[12] and then showed how Jesus went to the cross to be despised in our place.

He examined the capital crimes in the Old Testament—adultery, murder, homosexuality, incest, and so on. The list is long. Then he discussed how Jesus went to the cross to take the capital punishment that our crimes deserve. He emphasized sin in its various expressions, but in each case he used his congregation's bankruptcy in sin to unfold the glorious love of God. At the cross we see the horror of our sin, the love of God, and his infinite grace for sinners. It is all very humbling and very edifying.

A heightened sense of what the cross says about our sin and God's love is one crucial way by which we can measure the intensity of God's presence in our congregation. The closer God draws, the deeper we will feel our sin, our humility, and the depths of God's love. Whenever true revival comes, God's people are profoundly and joyfully humbled.[13] Church historian Iain Murray writes:

> The fact remains, that there has been an element present when the gospel has made its swiftest advances in the world that is notably uncommon today, namely, the fear of God. Not only the experience, but the very words have all but disappeared. . . . Wheresoever God works with power for salvation upon the minds of men, there will be some discoveries of a sense of sin, of the danger of the wrath of God.[14]

Ironically, as we have repeatedly noted, the more fully people understand the bad news and the gospel remedy, the happier they get. Humble people are a happy people. Humble people are a joyful people. Humble people are a zealous people. Gospel-humility is the cure for apathy and lukewarmness. Humble people are a serving, loving people. Congregations with leaders who fear God, not man, emphasize these truths. These congregations are characterized by a tangible joy. No matter what text they preach from, effective pastors look for ways to help their congregations grow in humility, for ways to exalt God in all his grace, mercy, and love.

SUMMARY

Pastors who use the gospel to humble sinners and saints must first conquer the fear of man.

When we make the praise of men more important than the praise of God, we become susceptible to pragmatism.

God is more interested in our faithfulness to the message than the size of our congregations. Most congregations in the Bible were small.

We overcome the fear of man with two weapons. The first is a growing capacity to fear God. The second is love for God and man.

We should engage in personal evangelism, counseling, and preaching with the intention of humbling sinners while we simultaneously exalt the love, mercy, and grace of God. The bad news makes an important contribution in this process. We must conquer the fear of man to be faithful to this process.

9

The Power of a Humble Leader

There are no virtues wherein your example will do
more, at least to abate men's prejudice, than humility
and meekness, and self-denial.

—Richard Baxter[1]

The three lessons which a minister has to learn: 1.
Humility.—2. Humility.—3. Humility. How long are
we to learn the true nature of Christianity!

—Charles Simeon[2]

IN THE MIDDLE of a sermon, I impulsively noted the
failure of a neighboring church to practice my main point.
I spoke critically. Never mind the fact that the sin for which
I criticized that church was one that had plagued me for
the first twenty years of my Christianity. I had forgotten
my own weakness. Now all I could see was theirs. I was

surgically removing a speck from their eye, even while I had a log in my own.

The next day a trusted friend approached me. "I was distressed by yesterday's sermon. You spoke from a proud heart. I don't think it was right. Your example has done much to undo your teaching on humility."

As soon as he finished, the Holy Spirit's sweet conviction came. I was grieved. Although I often speak about the importance of humility, my example said the opposite. The next Sunday, I apologized to my congregation.

This is what the Puritan Richard Baxter (1615–91) had in mind when he wrote, "Our very business is to teach the great lesson of humility to our people; and how unfit, then, is it that we should be proud ourselves? We must study humility, and preach humility; and must we not possess and practice humility? A proud preacher of humility is at least a self-condemning man."[3]

How and why to not be a "proud preacher of humility" is the subject of this final chapter. Before a Christian can produce humility in others, he or she must model it. Is anything more incongruous than a Christian who is not pursuing humility trying to help others become humble? From the obvious answer to this question I want to draw five crucial applications.

- First, the pursuit of humility is a battle.
- Second, intellectual pride will tempt pastor-scholars.
- Third, spiritual pride will tempt the zealous leader.
- Fourth, selfish ambition will tempt the effective leader.
- Fifth, pride in gifting will tempt the talented leader.

Christians who want to help others grow in humility put these symptoms of pride to death on a daily basis.

FIGHT FOR HUMILITY

First, the pursuit of humility is a battle. We must aggressively contend with the devil for any gains in humility. The devil is proud, and he wants to mold us in his image.

Humility makes us effective. This is why the devil hates it. Morphing us into workers "having the appearance of godliness, but *denying its power*" (2 Tim. 3:5) is his dark agenda. The easiest way to accomplish this is to lead us into pride. Peter exhorts us, "Be sober-minded; be watchful. Your adversary the devil prowls around like a roaring lion, seeking someone to devour. *Resist him*, firm in your faith" (1 Peter 5:8–9).

The symptoms of this sin are many. Pride has a foothold in our flesh, so the temptation to it is natural. The evil one will take that sinful tendency and try to drive us into intellectual pride, spiritual pride, selfish ambition, or pride in our gifts and talents.

INTELLECTUAL PRIDE

The first symptom of pride is intellectual. Pride tempts those zealous for knowledge. An aspiring leader pursues knowledge, but he does so to gain the respect of others. His learning morphs into a distorted thing. Because the devil knows this he will push and drive this process.

Knowledge is crucial: we can never have enough. But there is a right and wrong *reason* to pursue it. Hunger to know and love God is the right reason. Intellectual respectability—the admiration of others—is the wrong reason. It is an expression of pride. God will resist it.

Here lies the great danger of formal theological education. As knowledge and degrees accumulate, respect follows. The desire to gain more respect, or at least not lose what I have, becomes a great temptation. It must be resisted because it will

175

motivate gospel-compromise. To the mind of unbelief there is nothing respectable about the gospel, and there is no way to make it respectable without converting the unbeliever.

This sin is hard to detect. Here are some telltale symptoms. Do you delight in quoting authors that others find hard to read? Do you pursue advanced degrees to earn the admiration and respect of your peers? Do you talk about the books you read in order to gain the respect of others? If you went to a prestigious university, is your identity rooted in the institution? If it is not prestigious, are you ashamed of it? It would be better to be ignorant than to be a slave of intellectual pride.

"All of us possess knowledge," Paul observes:

> "Knowledge" puffs up, but love builds up. If anyone imagines that he knows something, he does not yet know as he ought to know. But if anyone loves God, he is known by God. (1 Cor. 8:1–3)

This passage implies three truths.

First, knowledge pursued for the right reasons enhances our status with God. The man who uses knowledge to better love and serve God will be "known by God." He will enjoy intimacy with God. That is because the pursuit of knowledge for the right reasons is an expression of humility, and God draws near to the humble.

Second, Paul implies that knowledge pursued for the right reasons deepens our contact with reality. It has a humbling effect. True knowledge makes us feel ignorant. By contrast, knowledge pursued for the wrong reasons makes us proud of our knowledge.

Third, Paul implies that knowledge pursued for the right reasons produces love. It builds other people up. But knowledge pursued for the wrong reasons produces arguments, quarreling over theological minutiae, and endless splits and divisions.

The crucial test, then, is this: What is the *effect* of your learning? Measure yourself! Does it make you feel small, ignorant, sinful, and needy; or does it make you self-satisfied, proud of your erudition, and convinced that you are wise, certainly wiser than most?

Intellectual pride renders entire denominations useless. It sucks spiritual power and vitality out of seminaries and Bible schools, it leaches the life out of Bible studies, and it renders many "doctors" impotent. Doctorates of ministry are useful if sought for the right reason, but if sought, even partly, to obtain prestige, they can be an obstacle to the gospel. It is better to be without them than suffer this sin.

Worst of all, intellectual pride replicates itself. Students of the proud become proud (Matt. 23:15).

The pursuit of God's power and the pursuit of intellectual respectability can be mutually exclusive. You can have proud intellectual impotence or intellectually humbling power, but you can't have both.

On the other hand, the fear of intellectual pride should not discourage the pursuit of knowledge. Little good occurs in the church without a profound and earnest cultivation of the intellectual life. Knowledge is the fuel that feeds the spiritual fire that glows in the heart of God's servants. But we must be continually watchful. Humbling is always the effect of true knowledge. "Such is the nature of grace, and of true spiritual light," wrote Jonathan Edwards, "that they naturally dispose the saints in the present state, to look upon their grace and goodness little, and their deformity great. . . . All true spiritual knowledge is of that nature, that the more a person has of it, the more is he sensible of his own ignorance."[4]

There is an insidious temptation against which we should be ever vigilant and that the church has struggled to overcome for two thousand years. God raises up a leader. He starts an organization. It could be a college, denomination, or mercy ministry. He rightly emphasizes knowledge and learning. Those who work with him also pursue learning for the right reasons. The next generation pursues knowledge, but the motives are not as pure. The third generation capitulates to the lust for intellectual respectability. It is truth decay, and the corrupting agent is the lust for respectability. The Christian wants to be loved and admired. In his book *Evangelicalism Divided*, Iain Murray shows the corrupting power of the lust for intellectual respectability. During the latter half of the twentieth century, many Christian scholars, on both sides of the Atlantic, started well, but the lust for the respect of their academic peers eventually seduced them.[5]

The gospel is the remedy. The cross, not knowledge, must always be our identification. The cross is never intellectually fashionable. You must be growing in humility to preach it, and its proclamation will increase your humility. The offense of the cross is the first casualty of the lust for intellectual respectability. Learn, study, and grow in the knowledge of God, but always scrutinize your motives.

SPIRITUAL PRIDE

Another closely related sin is spiritual pride, the secret conceit that, because we are smarter or more intimate with God, we and our church (or denomination) are God's favorites. This sin seduced me for many years. *If the other churches would only obey the Bible as we do, they would enjoy the special relationship with God that we have. Because we have _____, we are God's favorites.* This attitude caused me to look down on other churches. The more spiritual I felt, the more carnal I actually became. Pride is blindness, and to this sin I was oblivious. In his kindness God showed me my error. Over a period of years, this sin has slowly diminished. For that I am deeply grateful.

The Pharisees looked down on those who were not as spiritual as they. To the poor man born blind, they said, "You were born in utter sin, and would you teach us?" (John 9:34). The first symptom of spiritual pride is uncorrectableness. How can someone so obviously "spiritual" receive correction from a mere commoner? Here is a test. Can you accept criticism from your children, or your spouse?

A second symptom is control. Spiritual pride wants to control others. It is a first sign of cultic activity. *How could someone leave our church for that inferior congregation across town? They will miss out on what God is doing.* So we reject those who leave, or guilt-manipulate them into staying.

Spiritual pride was Satan's sin. It is his most potent weapon. It was the sin of the Pharisees. Publicly, sexual or financial scandals bring most leaders down. But spiritual pride, a secret sin, is even more deadly. The difference is that we put up with spiritual pride. A man can minister for years completely unaware of its presence, and almost no one will remove him from leadership because of it. In fact, by this sin the devil can effectively weaken a pastor, rendering him mostly ineffective. Why? The devil knows that God resists the proud. He knows that God will resist any Christian leader who doesn't pursue humility.

God will resist him by withdrawing spiritual power. Most will not notice. Some chemical weapons are odorless and tasteless, but they are still deadly. In the same way, a proud leader may be a man of outward integrity, even attracting others to his "morality," all the while infecting them with the same "spiritual pride" that has rendered him useless. The Pharisees had this outward morality. They even tithed their spices. But Jesus condemned them. "Woe to you, scribes and Pharisees, hypocrites!" warned Jesus. "For you travel across sea and land to make a single proselyte, and when he becomes a proselyte, you make him twice as much a child of hell as yourselves" (Matt. 23:15).

179

An evangelist from India took a rock from a Tibetan river. It was smooth and beautiful. He cracked it open to reveal a dry, dusty interior. "This is American Christianity," he said. "It looks good on the outside, but inside it is dry and hollow."[6] His words describe the leader oppressed with spiritual pride—moral and upright on the outside, but proud and conceited on the inside. He is dry and hollow. God has withdrawn his power.

As with intellectual pride, those who are not trying to put spiritual pride to death will find it difficult to help others grow in humility.

SELFISH AMBITION

Another symptom of pride is selfish ambition. Ambition is good as long as it is unselfish, as long as it is ambition for God's glory. This was the aspiration of John the Baptist. At the height of his popularity and influence, he lay down his ministry and reputation, a ministry for which he had waited all his life, but that he had exercised for only six months. "He must increase, but I must decrease" (John 3:30)—and with these words John retreated into the background.

Selfish ambition is a passion for my own glory at the expense of God and others. It is hard to see selfish ambition in ourselves. We assume that our ambition is unselfish. Here are symptoms to help us. Am I happy when another pastor's church doubles in size? Am I pleased when people leave my church to join his? Do I rejoice when people leave my Bible study for another? Am I delighted when revival comes to a church across town rather than mine? Am I thrilled when the elders give someone else the ministry that I have always wanted? Do we share the attitude of Paul?

Some indeed preach Christ from envy and rivalry, but others from good will. The latter do it out of love, knowing that I am put here for the defense of the gospel. The former proclaim Christ out of rivalry, not sincerely but thinking to afflict me in my imprisonment. What then? *Only that in every way, whether in pretense or in truth, Christ is proclaimed,* and in that I rejoice. (Phil. 1:15–18)

Dave Harvey tackles selfish ambition in his book *Rescuing Ambition.* He writes, "One great measure of our humility is whether we can be ambitious for someone else's agenda. Not just tolerate and accommodate the goals of those over us, but adopt their vision, promote and pursue their dreams. Our willingness to make others a success is a great measure of the purity of our ambitions."[7]

Pride in numbers is another expression of selfish ambition. Whether conducting a Bible study, leading a local congregation, writing books, or hosting a radio ministry, every Christian leader faces the temptation to measure his success by numbers. This sin becomes even more deadly when we measure God's *favor* by our numbers.

But the only legitimate measure of God's favor is *faithfulness.* As we have seen, when measured by numbers Jesus was a failure. On the day of Pentecost only 120 remained, but because he was "faithful" (Rev. 1:5), the Father exalted him and gave him the name above all names (Phil. 2:8–11). "Biblically," observes Mark Dever, "we must realize that the size of what our eyes see is rarely a good way to estimate the greatness of something in the eyes of God."[8] Repeatedly Jesus reminds us that God measures greatness by lowliness, humility, and servanthood.

Search your heart. Are you faithful to declare the whole truth, even offensive truth? Are you motivated by the fear of God or the fear of man? Are you willing to make the hard decisions that offend people? Do you fear your followers or God? Do you practice church discipline without partiality? If selfish ambition controls you, you will probably give the wrong answers to these questions.

We have reason to boast, but it is not in our numbers. "Far be it from me to boast except in the cross of our Lord Jesus Christ, by which the world has been crucified to me, and I to the world" (Gal. 6:14). The cross is the boast of the humble. It is a great mistake to glory in anything else, especially the number of followers that we attract.

PRIDE IN GIFTS

Finally, there is always the temptation to be proud of our spiritual gifts. If all else fails, the devil will try to drive us in this direction. We have all watched the athlete pound his chest on TV and exclaim, "I am the greatest. I am the best. No one can compete with me!" We find this repulsive, and we should. The reason it bothers us is transparent. The athlete is taking personal credit for a gift. His athletic ability is God's gift. He did not create it or give it to himself. He could have been slow and clumsy. A grandson receives a $1,000 gift from his grandfather and then says to a friend, "Look at me. I have $1,000. You don't have $1,000. What is wrong with you? If you were as good as me, you would have $1,000." That is what pride in our gifting looks like. It is especially ugly to God, the Giver. C. H. Spurgeon (1834–92) and George Whitefield (1714–70) are good examples of men who faced this temptation and overcame it.

So great were Spurgeon's oratorical gifts that before he was twenty-one he regularly preached to crowds in excess of five thousand, and he would have preached to more if there had been a building in London large enough to hold the throngs. He possessed an amazing gift of public speaking, and to his gift God added spiritual power. Even more amazing was Spurgeon's constant pursuit of humility. Reflecting back on his youth, he wrote:

> When I first became a pastor in London [about age 20], my success appalled me, and the thought of the career which it

seemed to open up, so far from elating me, cast me into the lowest depths. Who was I that I should continue to lead so great a multitude? . . . It was just then that the curtain was rising upon my life-work, and I dreaded what it might reveal.[9]

Spurgeon constantly credited his success to God and his mercy. He was convinced that his talents were "gifts" given for the edification of the church. He did not boast in his abilities. For this reason God used him greatly, and his influence continues today.

George Whitefield was similar. In 1736 at the tender age of twenty-two, he wrote in his diary: "Last Sunday I preached my first sermon. . . . Curiosity drew a large crowd. . . . The sight at first over-awed me. . . . As I proceeded, however, I perceived *the fire kindled.* . . . I trust I was enabled to speak with some degree of gospel *authority.*"[10]

The "fire" and the "gospel authority" to which he referred were the presence and power of the Holy Spirit. He would become very accustomed to this fire, for it would accompany him, with varying degrees of intensity, for the rest of his life. Such was its force that when the bishop heard that Whitefield's first sermon had driven fifteen people "mad" (a description of deep and profound conviction of sin), the bishop is reputed to have wished that they would stay "mad" until at least the following Sunday.

Before age twenty-five, Whitefield was preaching to crowds in the open air of up to fifty thousand with tremendous effects.[11] In light of these successes, he needed great humility, and God kept him humble. About this time he made an entry in his diary: "Every week I cry out, 'My leanness! My leanness!' 'Surely I am a worthless worm,' 'I am vile, I am vile, is all I can say to God or man,' 'I do not deserve even the rank of a common soldier in Christ's army,' and 'I cannot bear to live at this poor dying rate.' "[12]

Despite enormous natural gifts, both Spurgeon and White-field pursued humility. For this reason God used them. They continually reminded themselves that they had not created themselves or given themselves their talents. Rather, their abilities were for God's church. Their intellectual powers (Spurgeon was reading John Owen in grade school), their oratorical gifts, and the amazing spiritual power that frequented their ministries were all *from* God. They memorized Scriptures such as Romans 11:36: "For from him and through him and to him are all things. To him be glory forever." Their talents were gifts *from* Christ, they were empowered *through* Christ, and on the day of judgment those who possess them will give an accounting *to* Christ for their use.

Every humble heart possesses this same conviction. They lie prostrate in the dust, sensitized to their future accounting, and knowing that the accounting will be made according to their gifts. "Everyone to whom much was given," warned Jesus, "of him much will be required, and from him to whom they entrusted much, they will demand the more of him" (Luke 12:48). "Not many of you should become teachers, my brothers, for you know that we who teach will be judged with greater strictness" (James 3:1).

What is your gift? Are you a teacher, preacher, administrator, counselor, musician, pastor? Are you brighter than average? Do you relate to people easily? Are you clever? Maybe your gift is in the athletic realm or you are a good listener. Maybe it is acting. It matters not. When you take credit for your achievements and abilities, or lust for those that belong to another, you act from pride. Fear God and repent! God humbles the proud but gives grace to the humble. As Matthew Henry observed:

> It is God's prerogative to say, *I am that I am*; it is our privilege to be able to say, "By God's grace we are what we are." We

184

are nothing but what God makes us, nothing in religion but what his grace makes us. All that is good in us is a stream from this fountain. Paul was sensible of this, and kept humble and thankful by this conviction; so should we.[13]

HOPE FOR PROUD CHRISTIANS

As we mentioned in the first chapter, the first sign of pride is the conviction that I am already humble, certainly more humble than most. Remember, pride is spiritual blindness, and the first thing the proud are blind to is their pride. By contrast, the first sign of humility is a growing conviction that I am proud coupled with a growing hatred of that pride. Humility is the ability to perceive spiritual reality, and the first thing the humble see is their own pride.

If this is true, we all agree that we are fatally flawed with pride. I am sure that many reading this feel good about their humility. This means that you might have a problem. Thankfully, God has a glorious solution. It has five aspects, and each finds its consummation in Christ.

First, Jesus was humbled in our place. Repeatedly, Scripture promises us that God humbles the proud but exalts the humble.[14] Therefore, the proud must be humbled. It is an immutable spiritual law. This means that the proud will not get exalted into heaven. Instead, they will spend eternity humbled by God in hell. In fact, it is safe to say that even if the proud could go to heaven, they would not like it.

Therefore, atonement for pride needs to be made. Because our pride is infinitely offensive to God, it must receive an infinite humbling. It happened in an astonishing way. Jesus descended an *infinite* distance to save us. I say "infinite" because the distance between an infinitely exalted state and this finite world is an infinite distance. When we believe the gospel, our faith unites us to Christ, and his infinite humbling becomes

185

ours. Despite our penchant for daily arrogance, God now sees believers clothed with the infinite humility of his Son. This qualifies us for the infinite exaltation that Christ deserves for eternity. How great is the love of God!

Second, Jesus atoned for our pride by going to the cross. God poured out all of his hatred for our pride on his Son. Only death by slow, tortured agony was adequate to satisfy God's justice. Only the cross was adequate to quench God's wrath for our arrogance. In summary, God so loved the world that he solved our pride problem by sending his Son to become our humility. He also sent his Son to satisfy his own fierce anger for our arrogance.

Third, the life and death of Christ motivates us to pursue humility. After comparing our humility with that of Christ, so eloquently described in Philippians 2:5–11, no one will claim to be humble. Meditating on Christ's humility, however, will motivate proud Christians to hate their pride and earnestly pursue humility. The cross motivates that pursuit. Jesus' infinite descent gives us a graphic picture of the humility needed to earn God's favor. It is completely beyond us. In addition, Jesus' bloody death communicates God's infinite hatred of our pride. This prompts us to fear God and flee self-exaltation.

Fourth, our Father's willingness to send his Son to death on a cross in order to atone for our pride should astound us. He did this for enemies, not friends. His action demonstrates a love that is off the charts, a love that Paul says "surpasses knowledge" (Eph. 3:19).

Finally, because he loves us, God helps proud believers grow in humility. The church needs spiritual power to reach the lost. As we have seen, God empowers the humble. That is why, before using men and women, God often humbles them. God restored and used Job only after he said, "I despise myself, and repent in dust and ashes" (Job 42:6). God commissioned Isaiah only after he lamented, "Woe is me! For I am lost; for I am a man of unclean lips, and I dwell in the midst of a people of unclean lips" (Isa. 6:5). God used Peter only after the humbling that followed his threefold denial of Jesus (John 21:15–19).

There was a time when all this was taken for granted. "The man that understands the evil of his own heart, how vile it is," noted John Owen (1616–83), "is the only useful, fruitful, and solidly believing and obedient person."[15] If Owen was right, then humility should be the aim of both seminary training and pastoral apprenticeship. It should be the goal of both teacher and disciple. In the rush to get the appropriate academic training finished, however, this aspect is often overlooked or minimized.

In summary, there is grace for the proud. There is hope for the proud. There is mercy and love for proud sinners such as you and me. We need to live in that hope, bathe in that grace, and saturate ourselves in God's love even as we pursue a life of humility for the glory of God.

SUMMARY

Although we should pursue humility with all our hearts, those who know themselves see the pride that still lurks in their thoughts, attitudes, and motives. We who teach the importance of humility should model it. When we emphasize the importance of humility, but speak or act with pride, it sends a conflicting message. This will happen with the best of us. How much worse the damage when we are not aggressively pursuing humility!

Those who pursue humility recognize the constant nature of the spiritual warfare in which they engage. The devil's stealth weapon is pride. Those who serve the church in a leadership capacity are especially susceptible to his wiles. It is a respectable sin. Though few will call you on it, God will resist it. Christian leaders are especially vulnerable to intellectual pride, spiritual pride, selfish ambition, and the temptation to take pride in our gifts.

I pray that God will use this book for his glory. We are all proud sinners. We need light to see this truth. My heart longs to see God's people use the gospel to humble themselves and those to whom they minister. It takes courage and conviction to do this. It means helping others enter into the love of God by taking them through the door of God's wrath, the truth about final judgment, and the sinfulness of sin in order to showcase the glory of God's grace and love. But for those willing to do this, humility will be the end. The rewards are great, for God dwells with the humble.

May God give us all the courage to do this.

Amen!

Notes

Preface

1. William Law, *A Devout Call* (Rio, WI: Ages Software, 2000), CD-ROM, 192–93.

2. Stuart Scott, *From Pride to Humility* (Bemidji, MN: Focus, 2002), 2.

3. James Edwards, *Is Jesus the Only Savior?* (Grand Rapids: Eerdmans, 2005), 4.

4. David Wells, *The Courage to Be Protestant* (Grand Rapids: Eerdmans, 2008), 19.

5. Ibid., 45.

6. Handley Moule, *Charles Simeon* (1892; repr., London: InterVarsity Fellowship, 1965), 52.

7. I recognize that in a very broad sense, the entire book of Romans is about the gospel. Yet Paul succinctly sums up man's essential problem and God's glorious solution in Romans 1:16–3:26. The rest of Romans is fundamentally a proof of these assertions and application of them to daily life.

Part One

1. William Law, *A Devout Call* (Rio, WI: Ages Software, 2000), CD-ROM, 192–93.

Chapter One: "There It Is"

1. Quoted in "The Present Revival of Religion in New England," *The Works of Jonathan Edwards,* vol. 3 (Albany, OR: Ages Software, 1997), 104.

2. I know many faithful readers do not believe that God speaks to people today through any medium other than the Bible. I agree with them that the canon of Scripture was closed in the first century, and that it is against all the rules to add anything to the Bible. But I do not agree with them that communications from God through dreams, visions, and sometimes God's audible voice are additions to Scripture. Of course, all of these can be counterfeited by the devil or the flesh, and this raises a host of questions, too many and too complex to deal with in a note. My best understanding is that this position (cessationism, i.e., the belief that miracles and gifts of the Spirit ceased when the canon of Scripture was completed) is held for philosophical and traditional reasons, but not because of clear, solid biblical exegesis. Having said this, however, I also affirm that I love and honor my cessationist brothers and sisters.

3. Jonathan Edwards, *The Works of Jonathan Edwards*, vol. 1 (London, 1834; repr., Edinburgh: Banner of Truth, 1974), 294 (emphasis mine).

4. C. S. Lewis, *Mere Christianity* (New York: Macmillan, 1960), 109, 114.

5. For further light on this statement, see 1 Sam. 2:30; 2 Chron. 36:15–16; Prov. 1:7; 13:13; 14:2; Matt. 6:24.

6. Cornelius Plantinga, *Not the Way It's Supposed to Be* (Grand Rapids: Eerdmans, 1995), 82.

7. R. C. Sproul, "The Pelagian Captivity of the Church," *Modern Reformation* 10, 3 (May–June 2001), http://www.modernreformation .org/default.php?page=articledisplay&var1=ArtRead&var2=383&var3=issuedisplay&var4=IssRead&var5=40.

8. Jonathan Edwards, *The Works of Jonathan Edwards*, vol. 2 (Rio, WI: Ages Software, 2000), CD-ROM, 925 (emphasis mine).

9. John Flavel, *The Works of John Flavel*, vol. 1 (London, 1820; repr., Edinburgh: Banner of Truth, 1982), 226.

10. See C. J. Mahaney, *Humility: True Greatness* (Sisters, OR: Multnomah, 2005); Andrew Murray, *Humility: The Beauty of Holiness* (Feather Trail Press, 2009); Wayne Mack, *Humility: The Forgotten Virtue* (Phillipsburg, NJ: P&R Publishing, 2005).

Chapter Two: Convincing the Patient
1. C. S. Lewis, *Mere Christianity* (New York: Macmillan, 1952), 114.

2. C. S. Lewis, *God in the Dock* (Grand Rapids: Eerdmans, 1970), 202.

3. Raymond Ortlund Jr., *When God Comes to Church* (Grand Rapids: Baker, 2000), 208.

4. Stuart Scott, *From Pride to Humility* (Bemidji, MN: Focus, 2002), 2.

5. David G. Myers, *Social Psychology*, 5th ed. (New York: McGraw-Hill, 1996), 58–60.

6. David G. Myers, *The Inflated Self* (New York: Seabury, 1980), 5–43.

7. Myers, *Social Psychology*, 55–56.

8. Ibid., 53–55.

9. Dave Barry, *Dave Barry Turns 50* (New York: Crown, 1998).

10. Quoted in Paul Johnson, *Intellectuals* (New York: Harper and Row, 1988), 107.

11. Cornelius Plantinga, *Not the Way It's Supposed to Be* (Grand Rapids: Eerdmans, 1995), 84, quoting *New York* magazine (June 8, 1992): 111.

12. "Oprah: A Heavenly Body," *U.S. News & World Report* 122, no. 12 (March 31, 1997): 18.

13. Myers, *Social Psychology*, 61–62.

14. Ibid., 65.

15. Edward Welch, *When People Are Big and God Is Small* (Phillipsburg, NJ: P&R Publishing, 1997), 32.

16. Ibid., 146.

17. Quoted in John Calvin, *The Institutes of the Christian Religion* (Philadelphia: Westminster Press, 1960), 2.2.11 (emphasis mine).

18. Ibid., 2.2.10.

19. Jonathan Edwards, *The Works of Jonathan Edwards*, vol. 1 (London, 1834; repr., Edinburgh: Banner of Truth, 1974), 294.

20. Lewis, *Mere Christianity*, 111.

21. D. Martyn Lloyd-Jones, *Joy Unspeakable* (Wheaton, IL: Harold Shaw, 1984), 240.

22. Mark Water (compiler), *The New Encyclopedia of Christian Quotations* (Grand Rapids: Baker, 2000), 512.

Chapter Three: Humbled by the Wrath of God

1. J. I. Packer, *Knowing God* (Downers Grove, IL: InterVarsity Press, 1973), 156. Chapter 15 is dedicated to an excellent discussion of the wrath of God.

2. Ibid., 149, quoting A. W. Pink, *The Attributes of God* (Grand Rapids: Baker, 1975), 82.

3. Leon Morris, *The Atonement* (Downers Grove, IL: InterVarsity Press, 1983), 153, 155.

4. D. A. Carson, *Love in Hard Places* (Wheaton, IL: Crossway, 2002), 42.

5. John Stott, *Commentary on Romans* (Downers Grove, IL: InterVarsity Press, 1994), 71.

6. For more on the connection between idolatry and spiritual deadness, see the excellent study of this principle by G. K. Beale, *We Become What We Worship* (Downers Grove, IL: IVP Academic, 2008). Those who worship false gods become like them—deaf and mute to God's Word. This results from God's active judgment. He seals the ears, closes the eyes, and deadens the human heart to his Word. This hardening and deadening is an expression of God's wrath. The principle appears repeatedly in the Old Testament and in Romans 1:18–32.

7. Quoted in Ewald M. Plass, ed., *What Luther Says: An Anthology*, vol. 2 (St. Louis: Concordia, 1986), 563.

8. David Powlison, "Understanding Anger," *Journal of Biblical Counseling* 14, 1 (Fall 1995): 42.

9. Roland Allen, *Missionary Methods* (Grand Rapids: Eerdmans, 1962), 70.

10. John Bradford, *The Writings of the Rev. John Bradford* (Philadelphia: The Presbyterian Board of Publication, 1842), 73.

11. Mark Dever, *Christianity Today* (May 2006): 38.

12. Iain Murray, *The Old Evangelicalism* (Edinburgh: Banner of Truth, 2005), 24.

13. For a detailed study of this concept, read the book by Steve Jeffery, Michael Ovey, and Andrew Sachs, *Pierced for Our Transgressions* (Wheaton, IL: Crossway, 2007).

14. For more details, read the excellent article in *The International Standard Bible Encyclopedia* (1939; repr., Grand Rapids: Eerdmans, 1976), 2:760.

15. William Farley, *Outrageous Mercy* (Phillipsburg, NJ: P&R Publishing, 2009), 30–31.

16. D. A. Carson, *Scandalous: The Cross and Resurrection of Jesus* (Wheaton, IL: Crossway, 2010), 70.

Chapter Four: Humbled by Final Judgment

1. T. David Gordon, *Why Johnny Can't Preach* (Phillipsburg, NJ: P&R Publishing, 2009), 59.

2. P. T. Forsyth, *The Cruciality of the Cross* (1909; repr., Carlisle, UK: Paternoster, 1997), 59–60.

3. Bruce Milne, *The Message of Heaven and Hell* (Downers Grove, IL: InterVarsity Press, 2002), 32.

4. J. I. Packer, *Knowing God* (Downers Grove, IL: InterVarsity Press, 1973), 143.

5. Jonathan Edwards, *The Works of President Edwards*, Vol. VI (New York: Converse, 1829), 106–25.

6. Edward Payson, *The Complete Works of Edward Payson*, vol. 2 (1846; repr., Harrisonburg, VA: Sprinkle, 1988), 327.

7. Jung Chang and Jon Halliday, *Mao: The Unknown Story* (New York: Knopf, 2005).

8. D. A. Carson, *Scandalous: The Cross and Resurrection of Jesus* (Wheaton, IL: Crossway, 2010), 70.

9. Paul Barnett, *The Message of 2 Corinthians: Power in Weakness*, The Bible Speaks Today (Downers Grove, IL: InterVarsity Press, 1988), 103.

10. Richard Baxter, *The Reformed Pastor* (1656; repr., Edinburgh: Banner of Truth, 1974), 143.

Chapter Five: Humbled by the Sinfulness of Sin

1. David Wells, *No Place for Truth* (Grand Rapids: Eerdmans, 1993), 179.

2. William Plumer, *The Grace of Christ* (Keyser, WV: Odom, 1853), 20.

3. D. A. Carson, *Scandalous: The Cross and Resurrection of Jesus* (Wheaton, IL: Crossway, 2010), 41.

4. Horatius Bonar, *God's Way of Peace* (Darlington, UK: Evangelical Press, 1990), 27.

5. "Literally, a monstrous cloth." Robert Jamieson, A. R. Fausset, and David Brown, *Commentary Critical and Explanatory of the Whole Bible* (Oak Harbor, WA: Logos Research Systems, 1997), CD-ROM. On this verse J. Alec Motyer writes, "Sin is the defilement which a fallen nature imparts to all we do. *Filthy rags* is (lit.) 'a garment of menstruation'; bodily discharges were considered a defilement,

193

because they were the 'outflow' of a sinful, fallen human nature. So, even what we might consider to be in our favour, *righteous acts*, partake of the defilement of fallenness." *Isaiah: An Introduction and Commentary* (Nottingham, UK: Inter-Varsity Press, 1999), 442–43.

6. Three is the biblical number of exclamation, and exactly three times the Bible refers to men as worms: here and at Psalm 22:6 and Isaiah 41:14.

7. William S. Plumer, *The Grace of Christ* (Keyser, WV: Odom, 1853), 23–24.

8. See Mark 12:30. That was the problem with Old Testament law. It couldn't "make *perfect* those who draw near" (Heb. 10:1), and it needed to.

9. Jung Chang and Jon Halliday, *Mao: The Unknown Story* (New York: Knopf, 2005).

10. Thomas Watson, *A Body of Divinity* (1692; repr., Edinburgh: Banner of Truth, 1958), 146.

11. D. Martyn Lloyd-Jones, *Studies in the Sermon on the Mount* (Grand Rapids: Eerdmans, 1959–60), 209.

12. R. C. Sproul, "The Pelagian Captivity of the Church," *Modern Reformation* 10, 3 (May–June 2001): 22–23, 26–29.

13. Plumer, *The Grace of Christ*, 20.

14. Iain Murray, *The Old Evangelicalism* (Edinburgh: Banner of Truth, 2005), 24.

Chapter Six: Humbled by Faith Alone

1. J. I. Packer, preface to *The Doctrine of Justification*, by James Buchanan (1867; repr., Edinburgh: Banner of Truth, 1961), vii–viii.

2. David Otis Fuller, *Valiant for the Truth* (New York: McGraw-Hill, 1961), 360.

3. Ibid.

4. Quoted in J. I. Packer, *Faithfulness and Holiness* (Wheaton, IL: Crossway, 2002), 23.

5. Cited by D. A. Carson in *Scandalous: The Cross and Resurrection of Jesus* (Wheaton, IL: Crossway, 2010), 39.

6. See John R. W. Stott, *The Message of Romans: God's Good News for the World*, The Bible Speaks Today (Downers Grove, IL: InterVarsity Press, 2001), 109.

7. Iain Murray, *The Old Evangelicalism* (Edinburgh: Banner of Truth, 2005), 89.

8. This is why Paul used such strong and stringent language for anyone who attempted to add any works to our qualification for salvation. Paul accused the Judaizers, who wanted to add circumcision, of "deserting" Christ and "turning to a different gospel," and called down God's curse upon them (Gal. 1:6–10). Later, in his letter to the Philippians he referred to these men as "dogs, . . . evildoers," and "those who mutilate the flesh" (Phil 3:2). Finally, in 2 Corinthians Paul referred to them again. In this case he called them "false apostles, deceitful workmen," and accused them of serving Satan by coming to God's people as "angel[s] of light" (2 Cor. 11:13–15). These are not the words of someone who thinks *how* one responds to the gospel is a secondary issue. Paul speaks aggressively because the gospel, the glory of God, and the salvation of men depend on how we respond to the good news.

9. Buchanan, *Justification*, 222.

Chapter Seven: Humbled by the History of Preaching

1. Iain Murray, *The Old Evangelicalism* (Edinburgh: Banner of Truth, 2005), 24.

2. Brian Edwards, *Revival! A People Saturated with God* (Darlington, UK: Evangelical Press, 1990), 112.

3. Ibid., 115.

4. R. Albert Mohler, "Forum: Relevance of the Trinity," *Southern Baptist Journal of Theology* 10, 1 (Spring 2006): 91.

5. James Buchanan, *The Doctrine of Justification* (1867; repr., Edinburgh: Banner of Truth, 1961), 153 (emphasis mine).

6. Alister E. McGrath, *Luther's Theology of the Cross* (Oxford: Blackwell, 1985), 153 (emphasis mine).

7. Roland Bainton, *Here I Stand* (New York: Abingdon Cokesbury, 1950), 63.

8. Ibid.

9. This is an English translation of the Latin title. The exact translation varies by translator.

10. Martin Luther, *The Bondage of the Will* (Grand Rapids: Revell, 2002), 319 (emphasis mine).

11. J. I. Packer and O. R. Johnston, introduction to *The Bondage of the Will*, by Martin Luther (Grand Rapids: Revell, 1957), 41.

12. Ibid., 47.

13. Ibid., 58.

14. John Calvin, *Institutes of the Christian Religion* (Bellingham, WA: Logos Software, 1997), CD-ROM, 2.2.11.

15. J. I. Packer, *A Quest for Godliness* (Wheaton, IL: Crossway, 1990), 149–50 (emphasis mine).

16. Ibid., 170 (emphasis mine).

17. Leland Ryken, *Worldly Saints* (Grand Rapids: Zondervan, 1986), 103.

18. Jeremiah Burroughs, *Gospel Fear* (1647; repr., Morgan, PA: Soli Deo Gloria, 1991), 54.

19. Jonathan Edwards, *The Works of Jonathan Edwards*, vol. 2 (1834; repr., Edinburgh: Banner of Truth, 1979), 7–10.

20. Jonathan Edwards, *The Works of Jonathan Edwards*, vol. 2 (Rio, WI: Ages Software, 2000), CD-ROM, 925.

21. Arnold Dallimore, *George Whitefield*, vol. 2 (Edinburgh: Banner of Truth, 1995), 518.

22. J. F. Thornbury, *God Sent Revival* (Darlington, UK: Evangelical Press, 1988), 91–92.

23. Handley Moule, *Charles Simeon* (1892; repr., London: Inter-Varsity Fellowship, 1965), 52.

24. Edward Payson, *The Complete Works of Edward Payson*, 2 vols. (1846; repr., Harrisonburg, VA: Sprinkle, 1987–88), 1:91.

25. Ibid., 1:132.

26. Ibid., 1:186.

27. Ibid., 2:327.

28. Ibid., 2:419.

29. Ibid., 2:v–xi.

30. Mark Noll, *The New Shape of World Christianity: How American Experience Affects Global Faith* (Downers Grove, IL: InterVarsity Press, 2009).

31. Jonathan Edwards, *The Works of Jonathan Edwards*, vol. 1, *Religious Affections* (1834; repr., Edinburgh: Banner of Truth, 1974), 294.

32. Paul Miller, *A Praying Life* (Downers Grove, IL: InterVarsity Press, 2009), 238.

33. Thornbury, *God Sent Revival*, 77.
34. Ibid., 233.
35. Wayne Mack, *Humility: The Forgotten Virtue* (Phillipsburg, NJ: P&R Publishing, 2005), 124, emphasis mine.
36. Edwards, *Revival!*, 115.

Part Three

1. Alexander Whyte, *Bunyan Characters, Third Series: The Holy War* (Edinburgh: Oliphant, Anderson, and Ferrier, 1902), 202, 243, quoted in Iain Murray, *The Old Evangelicalism* (Edinburgh: Banner of Truth, 2005), 36.

Chapter Eight: The Fear of Man Is a Snare

1. John Bunyan, "Acceptable Sacrifice," in *Works of John Bunyan*, vol. 6, (Rio, WI: Ages Electronic Publishing, 2000), CD-ROM, 258.
2. For more on how this change took place, read Nathan Hatch, *The Democratization of American Christianity* (New Haven, CT: Yale University Press, 1989).
3. D. Martyn Lloyd-Jones, *Studies in the Sermon on the Mount* (Grand Rapids: Eerdmans, 1959–60), 296.
4. See Arnold Dallimore, *Spurgeon: A New Biography* (Edinburgh: Banner of Truth, 1985).
5. Iain Murray, *D. Martyn Lloyd-Jones*, 2 vols. (Edinburgh: Banner of Truth, 1990).
6. Iain Murray, *A Scottish Christian Heritage* (Edinburgh: Banner of Truth, 2006), 248–51.
7. Wayne and Joshua Mack, *The Fear Factor* (Tulsa, OK: Hensley, 2002), 143.
8. Ed Welch, *When People Are Big and God Is Small* (Phillipsburg, NJ: P&R Publishing, 1997).
9. Ibid., 95.
10. C. H. Spurgeon, *The Treasury of David*, vol. 2 (Grand Rapids: Baker, 1978), 174.
11. Mark Dever, *Nine Marks of a Healthy Church* (Wheaton, IL: Crossway, 2000), 194.
12. Here are some examples: Anyone who commits intentional sin despises God (Num. 15:30). Goliath despised David (1 Sam. 17:42).

After seeing God, Job despised himself (Job 42:6). Michal despised David in her heart (2 Sam. 6:16). David despised God with his actions regarding Bathsheba and Uriah (2 Sam. 12:9). Esau despised the inheritance (Gen. 25:34). Israel despised God in the wilderness (Num. 14:23). God will despise the wicked (Ps. 73:20). Israel despised God's promises (Ps. 106:24). The fool despises wisdom and discipline (Prov. 1:7). The fool despises God's discipline (Prov. 3:11). A foolish son despises his parents (Prov. 15:20). Unpunished sin causes us to despise God (Eccl. 8:11). The sin of the people of Israel was that they despised God's Word (Isa. 5:24). Jehoiakim despised the Word of God (Jeremiah 36). The priests showed contempt for God by offering defiled food on the altar (Mal. 1:6–7). You will despise either God or money, but you can't love both (Matt. 6:24).

13. See the excellent historical study by Brian Edwards, *Revival! A People Saturated with God* (Darlington, UK: Evangelical Press, 1990).

14. Iain Murray, *The Old Evangelicalism* (Edinburgh: Banner of Truth, 2005), 3–4.

Chapter Nine: The Power of a Humble Leader

1. Richard Baxter, *The Reformed Pastor* (1656; repr., Edinburgh: Banner of Truth, 2005), 65.

2. Handley Moule, *Charles Simeon* (1892; repr., London: Inter-Varsity Fellowship, 1965), 65.

3. Baxter, *The Reformed Pastor*, 144.

4. Jonathan Edwards, *The Works of Jonathan Edwards*, vol. 1 (London, 1834; repr., Edinburgh: Banner of Truth, 1984), 297, 299.

5. For an excellent study of this idea with real-life twentieth-century examples, read Iain Murray, *Evangelicalism Divided* (Edinburgh: Banner of Truth, 2000).

6. This quote was supposedly attributed to the Indian evangelist Sadu Sundar Singh.

7. Dave Harvey, *Rescuing Ambition* (Wheaton, IL: Crossway, 2010), 105–6.

8. Mark Dever, *Nine Marks of a Healthy Church* (Wheaton, IL: Crossway, 2000), 13.

9. Arnold Dallimore, *Spurgeon: A New Biography* (Edinburgh: Banner of Truth, 1985), 52.

10. Arnold Dallimore, *George Whitefield*, 2 vols. (Edinburgh: Banner of Truth, 1970), 1:97 (emphasis mine).

11. See ibid. for more details.

12. Ibid., 2:519.

13. Matthew Henry, *Commentary on the Whole Bible*, Logos Software ed. (Peabody, MA: Hendrickson, 1994), comments on 1 Cor. 15:1–11.

14. Here are a few of the texts, some of which make the point directly, some indirectly: Ps. 138:6; Prov. 3:34; 15:33; 16:18–19; 18:12; 29:23; Isa. 57:15; Ezek. 17:24; Dan. 4:37; Matt. 5:3; James 4:6; 4:10; 1 Peter 5:5–6.

15. John Owen, *Sin and Temptation* (Sisters, OR: Multnomah, 1983), xviii.